GUADALUPE VICTORIA

GUADALUPE VICTORIA

His Role in Mexican Independence

Arthur L. DeVolder

Artcraft Studios
Albuquerque, New Mexico

Published by
Artcraft Studios
1005 Columbia Drive N.E.
Albuquerque, New Mexico 87106

 Design and composition by Barbara Hoon of New Mexico Editype.

To

John Gaw Meem,

eminent architect, historian

humanitarian and scholar

CONTENTS

ILLUSTRATIONS

PREFACE

When Señorita Emilia Martinez del Rio invited me to her country home in Cuautla, Mexico in 1945, we discussed the importance of the city in the Mexican revolution in 1812, and I first learned about Guadalupe Victoria and his interrment in the base of the Column of Independence on the Paseo de la Reforma, which I had admired in my walks around Mexico City.

It was not until I was doing graduate work at the University of New Mexico under Dr. Dorothy Woodward that I again encountered data about Victoria and did a seminar paper about him. It was not until 1972, however, that I decided to delve more deeply into the life of this man, and obtained a sabbatical from my work at the University to travel to Mexico and Europe on the trail of the first Mexican President.

The life of Victoria is a mixture of legend and fact and at times it is difficult to know where fact and legend blend. Victoria was adored by the masses and held in contempt by many of his peers; yet he was the only President of Mexico who completed his full term of office--as stipulated by the Mexican Constitution at that time of four years--in the first half century of Mexican Independence.

This book reflects the uncertainty of a nation emerging from a servile period under strict Spanish domination and the problems of self-rule that confronted such leaders as Guadalupe Victoria and his contemporaries. Most of the men involved had little experience with independent governmental practices and knew less about the republican rule which they chose.

The first fifty years of Mexican independence covered an era that ran the gamut from monarchy to republicanism--with a battle between centralists and federalists beset by rival groups of Masons who caused much dissension leading to rebellion--and then to liberal and constitutional governments which were beset by a continuing war with Spain. This affair was finally settled by treaty in 1836, but was followed by trouble with France which was cleared in 1838. Governments appeared to change overnight until it ended in absolute dictatorial rule.

During much of this turbulent period until his death in 1843, Victoria devoted his life to his country. Even to this day historians have not fully accredited his accomplishments in holding together an emerging nation in an unsettled time beset with greed, personal ambition and conflicting powers between the Spanish, the Criollos, the Church, as well as the peons and the rising strength of the Mestizos.

ACKNOWLEDGMENTS

Many people--too many to list--have aided me in many ways to gather and to interpret the material contained herein. I will name those whose contribution was of the most value and aided most in culling out much extraneous data. They are: Jack Rittenhouse of the University of New Mexico Press; Roland Dickey, former Director of the UNM Press; Troy Floyd, Emeritus, History Department, UNM, and Marshall Nason, Director, Latin American Center, UNM. Rewriting advice was given by Peter L. Welch, Editorial Writer, Rolm Corporation.

Ms. Laura Gutierrez-Witt of the Latin-American Collection, University of Texas; Richard H. Dillon of the Sutro Library, San Francisco; Edward Telesford of the Photographic Services of the British Museum; Ms. Erika J. Thickman, Manuscripts Department, The Historical Society of Pennsylvania; and Sra. Elsa Barberena B., former Associate Librarian of the Universidad de las Americas and now with the Universidad Nacional Autonomica de México did much to supply needed documents.

Recognition must be given to Senor Ramón Bela of the Fulbright Commission in Madrid who gave me letters of introduction to various librarians in Spain opening many doors such as: Real Academia de la Historia, Madrid; Sra. Carmen Guzman of the Archivo Historico Nacional, and the Archivo General de Indies and the Biblioteca Nacional. In Mexico items were obtained from various librarians in the Biblioteca Nacional, the Universidad Nacional Autonoma de México, the Museo de Chapultepec, the Archivo General de la Nacion, the Archivo del Estado de Veracruz in Jalapa and the Archivo del Ayuntamiento del Saltillo.

For some translation aid I am indebted to Ms. Stella Torres and Ms. Viola Luna Easley. For reproduction of photographs I must acknowledge the aid of Arthur Jacobson, also the staff of the Instructional Media Services of the University of New Mexico; and for the excellent design and composition of the manuscript my thanks to Ms. Barbara Hoon. Lastly, my deepest appreciation to my wife, Jean Elizabeth, fellow librarian and general research assistant, who acted as my secretary and general advisor and was patient in the many trying hours of translating and transcribing.

CHAPTER ONE

PROLOGUE

For over three hundred years the triumvirate of the nobility, the Catholic Church, and the Spanish merchants dominated the colonies of New Spain. Their incessant quarrels and maneuvering for power--regardless of the consequences to the populace--made pawns out of most of the residents of New Spain. The end result was a rising dissatisfaction by many of the people of the colonies.

The Criollos, colonial-born Spaniards, and the Mestizos, descendants of the Spanish-Indian union, began to protest the monopolistic controls over business and governmental activities by the Spanish merchants and the Church, which controlled enormous wealth and property in New Spain.

The few Criollos who had attained property in ranching or mining interests were allowed no power of self-government and could not participate in governmental controls which were pertinent to their interests. The Criollos had the added handicap of trying to keep subdued and under servile control the Indians and peons who worked the land and the mines. This was a serious problem as these hacendados and miners were subject to the constant encroachment of the Spanish merchants who were granted special favors and protection by the monarchy. The control of prices which resulted in small returns to the Criollos was a harassment since small profits meant even more demands on the abused peasantry.

The case of the Mestizos was even more dire, and they despaired of any freedom to rise above their restrictive class structure. Their small business and agricultural holdings were always in financial trouble and when they borrowed money the Mestizos inevitably ended up losing their income and property. The Church --always financially strong and autocratic in its attitudes--was a power of which to beware. In times of financial crisis it was willing to loan money to the small businessman and to the hacendado or rancher who had large land holdings, but the Church was equally rapid in foreclosing on all properties should there be any delinquency in payments.

The Criollo or Mestizo who entered the ecclesiastical field was also limited, because the highest offices were reserved for those Spaniards who found favor with the court of Spain. Local churchly endeavor or leadership qualities of these colonial bred ecclesiasts were stifled. The church controlled educational institutions and any lectures that might be construed as liberal ideology were suppressed and offenders were punished. The Spanish rein was held tightly over the residents of New Spain and any brash enough to protest were soon controlled or banished from their duties.

Toward the end of the eighteenth century, in spite of the censorship of the Church and government, liberalism was on the rise. Much of this was inspired by pamphlets and books smuggled into the country and by discussions held by visitors or returnees from Spain. The turmoil in Europe caused by the French Revolution and the growth of interest in new freedoms for man inspired by such writers as Jean Jacques Rousseau and his works including _Discours sur l'inégalité parmi les hommes_ and _Du contrat social_; and Charles Louis de Secondat Montequieu's _De l'Esprit des lois_ were widely read by scholars in the centers of learning in New Spain even though forbidden. The French National Assembly's _Le Déclaration des droits de l'homme et du citoyen_ as well as the works of the Encyclopedists were influencial in freedom of thought which the Spanish banned.[1]

Richard Eugene Bailey in his study of French culture and its influence on Mexican history in the eighteenth century comments that many of the French revolutionary ideas came to the borders of New Spain via New Orleans and that "although a knowledge of them was certainly not widespread among the Mexicans, they were at least known to the leaders of the revolt; Hidalgo was frequently charged by the Inquisition with having read prohibited French books. . . ."[2]

The deep-rooted discontent among the Criollos and the Mestizos reached a crisis in the last days of the eighteenth century, as they sought actively equal social and political power. The effort of the Spanish leaders in New Spain to keep the colonies isolated from the rest of the world was not succeeding.

The suppressed people were beginning to resent fully the tyranny of their local leaders and wanted relief from their autocratic dominance. The new ideas of freedom, equality and justice which stemmed from the independence of the United States from England, the fall of the monarchy of France in 1789, and the Napoleonic deposition of Charles IV from the Spanish throne in the early 1800s, all began to raise their hopes of throwing off the yoke of suppression which constantly regulated and intervened in their lives, education and political destiny.

Several uprisings in the start of the nineteenth

century were to prove unsuccessful. Among the first, quickly subdued, was that of Virrey Don José de Iturrigaray, who in a rather oblique manner, suggested independence for Mexico in order to save New Spain from Napoleonic power. The Virrey Iturrigaray had received secret instructions from the Cortes at Cádiz not to obey edicts from Madrid, but to make every effort to preserve New Spain for the exiled Royal family. In appealing to the Mexican people to aid him in this goal, he stated his refusal to obey the mandates from the French and asked the aid of the Mexicans in preserving the throne for Spain.

Mark Beaufoy, a French traveller and writer, wrote of this historic event: "This statement created a sensation, for the idea of depending on Mexicans was unheard of, the ideas creating the dawning of liberty and a national existence glimmered upon them . . . the parish priests, the lawyers, and the Criollos saw some chance of preference opening to them."[3]

The hope was short-lived as the wealthy Spaniards of the Audencia of Mexico, who feared the result of local autonomy, arrested Iturrigaray, relieved him from his post, and on September 15, 1808, shipped him back to Cádiz, Spain. About this time another uprising was led by Don Francisco Primo de Verdad y Ramos, a member of the Mexico City Council, who stated in a debate: "as there was no king, the sovereignty of the country rested on the people."[4] To quell this popular thought Verdad was arrested, led from the meeting chambers and jailed for sedition. Shortly after imprisonment it was reported that he had been found in the morning hanging by the neck from the end of a rope which was attached to a nail in the wall of his cell.[5] The convenient access of the rope and nail in his cell was never explained.

Another victim was Friar Melchoir de Talamentes, who was confined over a period of time to several jails after he was apprehended for publishing articles advocating the cause of independence. He was reported to have died of yellow fever April 1809 in the dungeons of the Castillo de San Juan de Ulúa in the harbor of Veracruz.[6]

Pockets of resistance to Spanish authority continued to rise and although most of these rebellions were rapidly aborted, it was quite evident that the smoldering resentment against the government and the Church was on the point of eruption.

CHAPTER TWO

EARLY DAYS OF THE REVOLUTION:

1810-1814

In a quiet secluded room at the Colegio de San Ildefonso in Mexico City, a law student put down his books and reflected on the news a fellow student had related to him.

A conspiracy against the government had been uncovered in the city of Dolores in which the Cura of the Church of Dolores had declared for independence. The parish priest, Hidalgo, had been part of a group that was dissatisfied with the government and had been conspiring for change. He had been upset over the refusal of the Spanish authorities to permit him to raise the standard of living and to start new industries for the Indians. He felt the only hope for redemption of slavery of his people was rebellion. Picking up the standard of Nuestra Señora de Guadalupe from his church and crying for freedom, he led his forces against the royalist army.

The fateful "Grito de Dolores" by the Cura Miguel Hidalgo y Costilla uttered on September 16, 1810 did receive some military support from Ignacio Allende and Ignacio López Rayón. Hidalgo chose the latter as his confidential secretary. Most of his following were Indians and peons ill prepared to meet in combat the royalist armies of Spain. It was estimated that at one time his followers numbered 80,000. However, the mob was no match for the royalist armies. Nor was the looting and slaughter which resulted from the uprising of this undisciplined horde conducive to success. The Criollos and Mestizos, though sympathetic to the cause of independence, were afraid of this unruly mob whose battle cry was "Viva Nuestra Señora de Guadalupe, muera el mal gobierno, mueran los gachupines."[1]

Hidalgo's ragged army had a few successes--taking the city of Querétaro and sacking it, and then attacking Guanajuato and overcoming the garrison there. However, for some reason, Hidalgo did not attack Mexico City although he marched his army to that city without too much opposition. Sheer numbers could have overwhelmed the garrison at the city. The day in attacking the city lost the battle for Hidalgo and within a short span of time the royalist armies--with their superior discipline and arms--soon dispersed the rebels. Hidalgo

1. El Real Colegio de San Ildefonso (Escuela Nacional Preparatoria), Mexico City, where Victoria Guadalupe attended the Law School from 1807 to 1811, from México, edited by Luis A. Herrera. Reproduced by permission of the Mexican Consulate, Albuquerque, New Mexico.

was captured, tried by the Inquisition and condemned to death with great dispatch. His companions met the same fate, with the exception of Rayón, who was to carry on the fight for independence.

The fight for freedom had whetted the appetite for freedom of some chieftains among the Criollos and Mestizos. They took advantage of the opportunity that had been presented and thought it wise to continue the rebellion. A number of them banded together and selected another priest, the Cura de Carácuaro, José María Morelos y Pavón to carry the banner of freedom. Ignacio Rayón, whom Hidalgo had apointed as his confidential secretary, agreed to carry on his duties and pledged his allegiance to Morelos.

Meanwhile, the Spanish Cortes met in Cádiz on March 19, 1812. On this day the Cortes approved a Spanish Constitution which gave some power of self-government to the colonies. The Constitution confirmed the show of freedom which the Mexicans were making in their own territory toward the goal of self-government. This was the same type of action that was evolving in the internal provinces of Spain in the attempt to set up a constitutional government in Cádiz in defiance of the Napoleonic power.

However, after seeing the results of the first attempts to snatch freedom by bloody rebellion, persons such as the student, Guadalupe Victoria, although interested in obtaining independence hesitated joining the movement until the leadership of Morelos was proven.

Yet, the fight for freedom was deeply instilled in many people, and it was to be a political adventure of the era born of expediency for the purpose of protecting New Spain from the grasping hands of Napoleon and French domination.

The Criollos of Mexico waited anxiously for the clarification of the Constitution of Cádiz for it was heavily influenced by the French Constitution and the ideals of liberty and equality. Although the Constitution of Cádiz was set up to thwart French control, it provided the spark which was to give to the middle classes of Spain a new political recognition and in turn create in New Spain an era that was to bring to the colony more than a decade of internal strife, an empire, and ultimately the birth of a republic.

All this new activity by the government at Cádiz gave strong support to Morelos who began to assemble, to organize, and to create a military discipline among the stragglers of Hidalgo's army. The raw recruits were disciplined and given the rudiments of army tactics; Rayón set about to organize a form of government establishing the Junta of Zitácuaro, which the Spanish felt threatened the powers of New Spain. The leaders in Mexico City assigned the duty of crushing this upstart government to the powerful Félix María Calleja del Rey. He attacked Zitácuaro after a fortnight of siege and on January 2, 1813 he entered the town; but the leaders of the rebellion had fled to Sultepec. The Spanish General Calleja captured many valuable papers in Zitácuaro and had them copied by his scribe, Humaña, and incorporated them in his reports to the Audencia. They detailed many facts about the rebel forces and included letters from a secret society called the "Guadalupes" who evidently were made up of many influential citizens of New Spain. However, the names were coded and Calleja could not identify the supporters.[2]

Many young students and leaders among the Criollos and Mestizos were interested in independence for México; but they had been repelled by the carnage of the undisciplined hordes which Hidalgo had led and they had held back their support. These persons had also been concerned with the excessive demands of Hidalgo who wanted too many reforms at once. These demands had included complete freedom from Spain, autonomy of local industry, confiscation of landed property, and freedom from slavery. His ideas had been too utopian for them to accept; therefore they had refused to support him.

Morelos's activities appeared to be more subjective and appealed to a wider audience. Among those who had hesitated to take part in the earlier rebellion was the young law student, Don José Miguel Ramón Adaucto Fernández y Félix. This young scholar was to become known in Mexican history as one of the most sincere fighters for freedom under the name of Guadalupe Victoria. Victoria's parents were Don Manuel Fernández and Doña Alejandra Félix. They were landowners and mining developers in the province of Nueva Vizcaya (now Durango, Mexico). The parents recorded his birth in the records of the Real Universidad de México. The records stipulate that he was born in the Villa de Tamazula in Nueva Vizcaya on September 29, 1785. Various authorities differ on the exact date, but Felipe Victoria Gómez, a descendant of Victoria's, substantiates this date in her publication about the revolutionary.[3]

Not much is known of Guadalupe Victoria's youth. A skimpy reference is given by José Fernando Ramírez, who states that the boy was orphaned at an early age and that he was reared by his paternal uncle, Agustín Fernández, cura of Tamazula. Evidently the cura, Fernández, was reluctant to broaden Victoria's education and he kept him in Tamazula and tutored him personally as time permitted. Eventually Victoria rebelled at this treatment and left his uncle's guardianship to go to the Colegio de San Nicolás in Valladolid (now Morelia). Later at the age of nineteen he matriculated for special studies in the Colegio de Durango. He is said to have given his legacy of 1000 pesos to his sisters and that he was destitute when he arrived at the Colegio de Durango.[4]

Victoria came under the protection of the Rector of the Colegio where he studied philosophy as well as tutoring the younger students in Latin. He was proficient in this work and advanced his ability in Latin with the scholars at the Cathedral Medianos. In his work and study he already showed signs of the tenacity, perseverance and willingness toward work which persisted to his last days.

Guadalupe Victoria showed his usual reticence and desire for privacy during his residency at Durango from 1805 to 1807 and continued this attitude when he left this city to matriculate to the Colegio de San Ildefonso in Mexico City to study law at the end of 1807. He was sent to San Ildefonso under the auspices of Don Baltazar Bravo de Castillo, father of one of the students Victoria had tutored at Durango.[5]

Guadalupe Victoria was proficient in his studies and was interested and capable in carrying out his assignments in military studies. His fellow students considered him rather odd and over-imaginative. He was very sensitive to the jibes of his companions and shunned their company. Victoria was interested in the development of the freedom attitudes of the people with whom he associated and followed details of the rebellion in the newspapers and in the talk at the Colegio. Though sympathetic to the ideals set out by Hidalgo, he kept silent when told of the successes of the revolutionary leader for he was repelled by the combination of rape, murder, and religious fanaticism practiced by the insurgent army. Many of the Hidalgo followers were peons held in check by the hacendados. The Criollos feared the mob violence would turn upon them. These were the persons with whom Victoria identified himself. They were the patrones who had aided him in his educational pursuits. He feared for their safety as well as his own.

Consequently, Victoria decided to continue his studies rather than join the battle at this time. However, he learned of Hidalgo's subsequent capture and execution, and the assumption of command of the rebel army by Padre José María Morelos y Pavón, who was a former student of the Colegio de San Nicolás and currently a cura of a small parish in a village in western Michoacán. Many glowing reports of the extraordinary character of Morelos came to the attention of Victoria. He learned of the disciplining of the bedraggled remnants of Hidalgo's army and of the change of tone in the ideology of independence as outlined by the new leader.

Guadalupe Victoria resolved to seek out this man, as he felt that this was the opportune time to join the rebel forces and to proclaim his support of the republican cause, and to work for the independence of Mexico. He left his studies and offered his services to Morelos just prior to the time the rebel leader marched into Cuautla in February 1812.[6]

The new recruit, Victoria, within a few days of his enthusiastic enlistment, nearly ended his army career before it got a good start. Morelos was out scouting with several of his troops to try to gauge the strength of his opponent, General Félix María Calleja. Inadvertently he traveled too far behind the enemy's lines and was soon surrounded by scouts of the opposing army. He was in danger of being captured when General Hermenegildo Galeana, with a group of brash young revolutionaries, including Victoria, went to the rescue. In the brief clash that followed Victoria was wounded by a ball in the thigh. Ignoring his pain, he fought with the group and they all managed to escape the enfolding trap and returned to the fortifications in Cuautla.

For several days Victoria was in serious condition since the wound became badly infected. The festering sore was treated by the famed surgeon, José María Cos y Pérez,[7] who managed to prevent gangrene from setting into the wound which might have led to amputation of the wounded soldier's leg. For about a week Victoria was in great pain, at times delirious and sometimes in a coma, but the diligent care of Dr. Cos soon brought him out of danger.

Victoria was an invalid during the famous siege of Cuautla by Calleja's forces from February 11 to May 1, 1812. Battered by cannonball fire from the Royalist army, the small group of rebels literally had most of the town destroyed around them. Food was scarce; even the domestic animals had been eaten in order to survive. Casualties were heavy, and starvation was facing the rebels. The fortifications were beginning to crumble, and it appeared unlikely that the rebels were going to be able to survive Calleja's onslaught.

Finally, realizing that to survive the remnant of the rebel army needed to evacuate Cuautla, Morelos marshalled his officers and explained a plan of action which would allow them to escape the ravaged village. In the dark of the night, passing through a small ravine and crossing a shallow river guarded by the enemy, the rebel army survivors crawled beyond the first entrenchment of Calleja's army. By the time the sleepy guards detected the activity, the rebels were able to escape by rapid dispersion of their troops. The group reassembled again several days later in Izucar, approximately twenty leagues from Cuautla. Among those who successfully left the city was Victoria. Though feverish and limping heavily from his slowly healing wound, he had managed to elude the enemy and to find his way to the rendezvous.

In the confusion which followed the discovery of Morelos's tactics, many of the Royalist troops had fired upon one another in the belief that the opposing forces were the enemy. This aided the rebels to flee to safety. Subsequently, Calleja's troops captured Cuautla which was undefended except by the severely wounded and the few civilian survivors. In anger Calleja ordered the indiscriminate slaughter of those remaining including the infirm, as well as the citizenry who had shown sympathy and support to Morelos and his followers.

After the rebel army reassembled at Izucar, they rested there for several months before continuing their campaign in the southern part of Mexico. Morelos divided his forces sending a contingency to Puebla and Veracruz to cut communications between the coast and Mexico City. With the remaining troops he set off for Oaxaca. He had a complement of approximately 5000 men when he set out on his new campaign. The officers designated by him at this time were Ramón Sesma, D. Victor, Miguel Bravo, José, Antonio, and Hermenegildo Galeana, Vicente Guerrero, Guadalupe Victoria, and Manuel Mier y Terán, who was in charge of the artillery.[8] The latter two had passed their muster under

Morelos's scrutiny and had been designated as "Jefes."

It was in Oaxaca that Victoria first received significant recognition, although versions regarding his actions vary greatly. One story has the sequence of events as follows: Morelos had called upon the Royalist troops--which he had under siege in Oaxaca--to surrender in three hours by midnight November 24, 1812. The demand was refused. The insurgent chief divided up his forces and surrounded the city, giving various of his leaders specific assignments as to the points of attack. At a pre-arranged signal all units moved toward the walls.

In one area the insurgent forces has spent nearly three hours trying to overcome the Juego de la Pelote, a point of fortification protected by a moat and drawbridge. Little headway was being made. With the drawbridge raised, the obstacle of the moat was formidable and gave pause to a straightforward assault. Victoria, impatient at the delay, when he heard the bells of the church of Santo Domingo ring in the pre-arranged signal --signifying the breaching of the walls of part of the city--threw his sword across the moat and said. "There goes my sword in pawn; I am going over to retrieve it." Sliding down the embankment he swam across the moat, reached his sword and cut the ropes to the drawbridge. Following his example the insurgent troops swarmed across the lowered bridge, capturing the defense post.[9]

However, Alamán writes that a firsthand report from Mier y Terán revealed that the Royalists of Soledad Fort fled the position at the drawbridge leaving behind only a sergeant to see to the protection of the bridge and the moat. Mier y Terán claims his artillerymen breached the moat and overran the fortifications leaving Victoria floundering in the mud of the moat.[10]

It was shortly after the capture of Oaxaca and the later campaign against Acapulco, that Victoria had--with a fervent devotion to the battle insignia of the Virgin and with a firm belief in the cause of liberty --committed himself to change his name to Guadalupe Victoria. His purpose was to honor the holy symbol of the patroness of the insurgents and to show subjection to Nuestra Señora de Guadalupe and to signify the strong belief he had in the ultimate victory of the insurgent army over Spanish domination.

Throughout his youth Victoria had close contact with men of the Church. His own uncle was a clergyman and had endeavored to interest the young man in following in his footsteps. Victoria had been educated in schools dominated by the Church, so it would not be unusual for him to show extreme devotion to Nuestra Señora de Guadalupe. His parents being devout Catholics would have influenced his thoughts in this religious symbol and encouraged prayer to the Mexican virgin.

Some of Victoria's colleagues had always felt that he was a rather odd young man and that his action in taking the pseudonym was in accordance with his nature. However, in later years, historians seem to be confused by the change and refer to him by several names: Manuel Félix Fernández, Juan Félix Fernández, and José María Fernández. His baptismal name has been verified as José Miguel Ramón Adaucto Fernández y Félix by Felipe Victoria Gómez.[11]

When, in his enthusiasm for the idea of adopting his new name, he mentioned his plan to Mier y Terán, the young officer ridiculed him and said a more suitable name would be "America Triunfo." This buffoonery by Mier y Terán disheartened and angered Victoria, who was sincere in his religious belief and his idealistic dream of a free Mexico.[12] The ultimate result of this rancorous remark by Mier y Terán was to create in the years following an animosity between the two which often prevented concerted action in the battles for independence and the creation of stability in various governmental actions.[13] In spite of the adverse criticism by Mier y Terán, Victoria assumed his new name with dignity and continued his services to Morelos who assigned to him more responsibility.

The capture of the city of Oaxaca from the royal commander, General Antonio González Saravia, gave Morelos additional strength as he had captured forty cannon, large amounts of provisions, and approximately 2000 fully equipped prisoners. This was a fortunate prize for the rebels, giving them a vast store of supplies to carry on their activities.[14]

After resting his troops and celebrating the Christmas season festivities Morelos marched on to Acapulco, arriving there in February 1813. Morelos believed the city would fall into his hands easily, but the port defenders were well supplied by sea and were able to hold the rebels at bay for many months until they finally capitulated in August 1813. The control of the south of Mexico was now complete and the independence army increased in importance and influence.

During this period of affluence, Morelos appeared more anxious for the welfare of his country than displaying his character as a military genius. He was the first to promote and to propose the formation of a civil government, and thereby gave unequivocal proof of his patriotism. He devoted himself to assembling a national congress composed of the Junta of Zitácuaro, representatives from Oaxaca, and others from provinces still under Royalist domination.

In establishing the Congress of Anáhuac in Chilpancingo on September 8, 1813, and later having an act of independence approved on November 18, 1813, Morelos established part of his goals. These included the abolition of slavery, distribution of the land, equality of rights for all citizens, and support of independence from Spain. He established a democratic republic including freedom from tyrannical subservience.[16] It is little wonder that he obtained complete support from Guadalupe Victoria for it appeared to him the attainment of the goals for which Victoria had pledged his life and sword.

Morelos also sought--as within reason for a clergyman--the monopoly of religion by the Catholic Church exclusive of others and the abolition of the Spanish rule with no intervention from any European nation.[17]

Although most of Morelos's followers favored the establishment of the Congress as the first step in Mexican independence, it appeared later to have been a grave error of judgment. According to Conder, the Congress thwarted Morelos's military plans, betrayed his movements to the enemy, passed capricious taxation to pay themselves salaries and gave conflicting orders to the scattered military chieftains which led to disunity and chaos. Within a short time, the strict discipline that Morelos had set up within his military structure was on the verge of collapse.

In giving the Constitutional Congress of Chilpancingo power over the military chieftains, Morelos lost control of his troops. He might have consolidated his gains first and then set up the congressional structure which could have created an economic, social and political entity. It was the opinion of historians in later studies of his government, that the constitutional assembly was not united and would not agree with the insurgent leader on his Sentimientos de la Nacion which led to ultimate dissolution of the congress, after his death.[19]

Establishment of the Congress, however, was the first major step toward independence and the beginning of a political entity and that is why he won support from Guadalupe Victoria, Vicente Guerrero, the Bravos, Galeanas and others who were concerned with the independence of Mexico.

However, the Cortes of Cádiz finally decided to give Calleja more power and removed Venegas, making Calleja the Virrey effective on March 4, 1813.[20]

One of Calleja's first acts was to ask for sufficient funds from the Cortes to adequately defend new Spain. His request was promptly denied and he was notified that the Spanish treasury was depleted because of the many problems it faced and that he would have to find his own resources in New Spain. Needing funds to refurbish his troops and supplies, Calleja solicited a loan of two million pesos from the local Spanish merchant/capitalists. He guaranteed them repayment by mortgaging the antiticpated income from taxes he was planning to impose upon the people. Realizing the consequences of an independent army's victory if Calleja could not hold back Morelos's troops, the Spaniards were more than willing to meet his demands, for they were deeply concerned with the many successes Morelos had been attaining in the southern area of the country. They did not have complete faith in Calleja because of the manner in which Morelos had eluded his army in Cuautla; but the choice open to them was to fall into the hands of the rebels or aid Calleja; and they felt that their future under rebel rule might not be too bright, so they chose Calleja.

Behind the formation of the government was the ideology of saving Mexico from French domination, moving away from Spanish rule and giving a governmental entity to the insurgents which would enable them to send out envoys for financial aid to further their goals. It was this type of incentive that kept Victoria and the other chieftains loyal to Morelos and to the cause of independence and freedom.

However, it is necessary to digress here to go back to the action taken by the Spanish government in the period when Iturrigaray had been removed as the Virrey of Mexico. The Audiencia of Mexico took over the government of New Spain until a new Virrey could be appointed. This was to take some time, and it was not until August 25, 1810 that Don Francisco Xavier Venegas --chosen by the Cortes of Cádiz--arrived in Veracruz. He had traveled on to Mexico City, entering the royal palace on September 14, 1810 just two days before the fateful declaration by Hidalgo. The Virrey Venegas wanted to quell the uprising, but he lacked full details on the coup and insufficient troops to take immediate and full action.

Finally Venegas called for reinforcements from San Luis Potosí. He placed at the head of the Royalist army the stern disciplinarian, General Félix María Calleja del Rey, who had been commander at San Luis Potosí. Calleja pursued the ragged hordes of Hidalgo and overcame them. He later fought against the newly disciplined fighters of Morelos, but the wily leader was not as easily overcome as his predecessor.

With the money obtained from the Spaniards, Calleja strengthened his army and placed it under the leadership of a young Criollo Colonel Augustín de Iturbide. The Royalist army was able to slow down some of the successes of the rebel troops in the latter part of 1813. On November 8, Morelos marched his army toward Valladolid, reaching the city on December 23. A large force was marshalled against him by Brigadier Ciriaco del Llano and Colonel Iturbide. Morelos's troops were weary from their long march and totally unprepared for the assault. They were routed from their defenses and some of the best regiments surrounded and the artillery captured. The remnant of the rebel army fled to Puruarán, where Iturbide again assailed the defenders, and captured one of the most intrepid fighters, Mariano Matamoros y Guridi y Oribe, on January 6, 1814. Matamoros was truly a great loss to the rebel army for he was one of Morelos's trusted officers. He had joined the army in 1811 and had been one of the major defenders against Calleja in the battle of Cuautla and one of the chief planners in escaping the siege there. He had also been at Oaxaca and Acapulco and was at that time appointed second in command of the rebel army by General Morelos, with the title of Teniente General. He had advised Morelos against making a stand at Puruarán but had been overruled. After his capture he was taken to Valladolid where he was placed on trial, condemned to death for treason and shot in the main plaza of that city on February 3, 1814. Morelos had attempted to ransom this insurgent hero; but Calleja in his usual uncompromising fashion did not listen to his pleas but had him condemned to death.

The Royalists were well supplied and confident of further victories, but they could not quell the drive for freedom. Calleja, in a letter to the Minister of Justice written on August 18, 1814, stated that the whole population in the outlying pueblos were bent on the attainment of an independent political existence in spite of the efforts of the Royalist troops to put down the rebellion. He also mentioned the activities of the "Guadalupes," a secret organization of men in the government who were aiding the rebels with information and money. He revealed that when headquarters of the rebels were seized in Puruarán, Tlacopepec and Pátzcuaro, he had obtained copies of letters from these traitors as well as names of the chief rebels, and correspondence with English, Anglo-Americans and with Santo Domingo natives in which they (the rebels) were seeking aid from these groups in furthering their revolutionary goals.[21]

The loss of Matamoros had been a disaster for the independents, but shortly thereafter other defeats were sustained. Miguel Bravo was captured and in spite of Nicolás Bravo's offer to exchange three hundred prisoners for his father, the elder Bravo was executed. Hermenegildo Galeana was the next fatality.[22] The Congress of the independents was driven from Chilpanzingo to the woods of Apatzingán, where it continued its labors and put forth a constitution in 1814.[23]

It established an Acta de Independencia severing all ties with Spain and establishing a government with powers to make alliances and treaties and to pursue war, and to seek recognition of independence from all nations in the world. The Congress sent out ambassadors and ministers to various governments to seek aid and establish treaties, especially in Europe. The chief officials of the Congress were Andres Quintana, Ignacio Rayón, José Manuel de Herrera, Carlos María de Bustamante, José Sixto Verdusco, José María Liceaga, and Cornelio Ortiz de Zárate.[24]

Francisco Bulnes, the Mexican historian, felt that the Constitution of 1814 set up at Apatzingán had merit and that the general ideas of liberty codified Mexican ideals; but it considered itself a political entity and existence it did not have. He felt it was neither valid nor effective.[25]

According to Lorenzo de Zavala, "José María Morelos believed it was time to form a national congress which would formulate a regular government which was the object for his struggles and sacrifice. . . ."[26] A history of Mexican law states: "Morelos' ideas were liberal ideas, a work brilliant and suggestive proclaiming the principles of equality, liberty and repect of the human person, enumerating carefully the rights of man and giving him legal protection, guaranteeing him the liberty of education, free expression of his thoughts and conscience and recognized the dignity of work of all men with all facilities of the government and within full protection of the law."[27]

These ideals were the reason why so many of the young Mexican criollos were willing to follow Morelos and sacrificed security and comparative comfort of education and the ease of city life for the rigors of the rebel campaign, rugged living in the mountains and desert and the stifling heat of the tropical jungle. Little did many realize that the following years were to be filled with heartbreak and disaster.

While Morelos and his chieftains held sway in Puebla, Guanajuato, Valladolid, Zacatecas, and Nueva Galicia, circumstances were beginning to change and toward the end of 1814 and the beginning of 1815, the Royalists brought in new recruits from Spain and their successes began to make serious inroads in the holdings of the rebels. The constant push against the rebels, aided by the addition of troops, fresh supplies, larger munitions and the trained disciplined soldiers made the insurgents retreat into the foothills and the mountains. The drive of the royalists came to Apatzingán and threatened the safety of the republican congress. Morelos, being aware of the danger of being surrounded, decided to move the group to hill-girded Tehuacán. He sent orders to the generals Nicolás Bravo, Manuel Mier y Terán, and Vicente Guerrero to come to his aid and escort the Congress to Tehuacán. Only Bravo appeared, as the orders to the other insurgent chiefs were intercepted.

Calleja's military leaders, acting upon the plans

which they had captured, sent troops to seize the Congress and Morelos. The Royalists encountered the republican troops, which were escorting the deputies of the Congress at Tezmalaca and engaged them in battle. The odds were overwhelming and Morelos was being badly mauled. Noting that defeat appeared inevitable, he commanded Bravo to withdraw with the deputies while he held the vanguard. "Go," he said, "protect the Congress; it matters not if I perish."[28]

Morelos was soon surrounded and capitulated to the Royalists, but Bravo succeeded in escorting the deputies in safety to Tehuacán, where they received a respectful welcome from General Mier y Terán. Yet how futile was Morelos's sacrifice for shortly afterward the congressmen began squabbling among themselves and with the rebel chieftains. There were several actions of the congressmen that created problems. One bitter argument was that the Congress levied funds to pay themselves regular stipends rather than divert the monies received to pay for supplies, munitions and troop needs. The chieftains further dissented with the attempts of the congressmen to take over complete military control from them and to control their movements. As many of these deputies had not participated in the danger of strife and were unaware of the effects of their conflicting orders which were creating confusion, the chieftains refused to follow their dictates and went their own way.[29]

General Mier y Terán was thoroughly discouraged by these inner conflicts and, with the approbation of Vicente Guerrero, marched on the deputies in their chambers and said: "Gentlemen, you are a set of asses and plunderers, living on contributions you have no right to levy. Begone, the chiefs of the patriot troops dissolve you."[30]

Although there was slight opposition to the dissolution of the Congress, there was some attempt to set up a triumvirate to rescue the republican body, but it failed. Justo Sierra, in writing about Mier y Terán's action, said that this "arbitrary dissolution of Congress was to prove fatal to the republican cause, for it resulted in the crushing defeat of the guerrilla leaders who refused to cooperate collectively. Others feeling the revolution was futile without Morelos's decisive leadership eventually began to capitulate to the new Virrey, Juan Ruiz Apodaca, who set up generous terms and full pardons for those who would surrender under the 'indulto.'"[31]

The execution of Morelos by the Royalist forces seven days after the dissolution of the Congress, on December 22, 1815, climaxed what appears to have been a futile attempt to set up a republic form of government to free Mexico from the imperialist yoke of Spain.

It also created fresh courage among the Spaniards in Mexico and the royalist armies who renewed their onslaughts with a new vigor.[32]

Bremauntz in writing about the social aspects of the trial and execution of Morelos states: "It is important to note that Morelos was tried not by a military tribunal, but by the Inquisition. He was condemned to death for his upholding the ideals of freedom proclaimed by such 'heretics' as Hobbes, Helvecia, Voltaire, Luther and other pestilent authors, deists, materialists, and atheists, apostates of the sacred religion, libertines, seducers and offenders of the majesty of human rights, enemies of the christianity and the church. . . ."[33]

According to Bremauntz Morelos was accused of communistic ideology which planned to deprive the rich, noble, the employees of the first order, criollos and gachupines of their money, and property, when in reality he wanted a just reward for the work of the peasantry and agrarian rights. He felt that "José María Morelos es el Precursor Revolucionario del Agrarismo en México."[34]

Without doubt Morelos had been influenced in the cause of humanism and freedom while at the Colegio de San Nicolás and was aware of the philosophies of the French Revolution, and the ideas of Rousseau, Charles de Secondat, the Baron de Montesquieu; these thoughts were expressed in his letters and the Sentimientos. It is not surprising that Virrey Venegas regarded him and his followers as formidable enemies. He said of the Padre: "Morelos is the principal Corifeo (leader) of the insurrection in every way and I say he is a man of genius, of major firmness, unmerciful and cunning."[35] Calleja was of the same opinion and declared: "Morelos is a Mahomet who promotes the insurrection with a passion and a feeling as vicious as that of the Musselman."[36]

CHAPTER THREE

YEARS OF SUCCESS AND DEFEAT:

1815-1818

After the battle of Oaxaca and service in Acapulco and the southern part of Mexico, Guadalupe Victoria was recalled by Morelos in the early part of 1814 and was sent to Veracruz as an assistant to Juan Nepomuceno Rosains to replace Juan Pablo Anaya, who was being sent to the United States as an envoy for the republican government. Anaya expressed his dissatisfaction with the new appointment feeling that this frail youth could not withstand the rigors of the guerrilla warfare that had been taking place in the province of Veracruz. Yet, Anaya felt that Rosains could handle the situation and since his appointment had been approved by the Congress with a strong recommendation from Morelos there was little he could do, although he felt that this young soldier did not appear strong enough to carry out any type of demanding military action.

The curly-haired, pleasantly countenanced Victoria was enterprising, and somewhat reckless; yet he had in the southern campaigns showed that he was cool and decisive in battle. With surprising energy and constancy he had accepted all the privations and sufferings along with his fellow soldiers and had carried through his activities with kindness, consideration and generosity which gained from his subordinates an extreme popularity and loyalty.

Victoria was in poor health when he arrived in the humid climate of Veracruz. The trip from southern Mexico had sapped some of his vitality. Of average height, he appeared somewhat frail and was rather timid in his approach to his new responsibilities. He had a slight permanent limp because of the wound he had received in the skirmish at Cuautla. It is not surprising that the young revolutionary made a poor impression on the people in the province when he presented himself to Rosains for duty.

Rosains was somewhat disillusioned with the new assistant, but was not overly concerned as he felt that the bad climate--coupled with the strong Royalist forces in the area--would soon rid him of this weakling and that Victoria's days were numbered. However, before many weeks the image changed. Victoria's guerrilla tactics and his skill in military logistics created a new high in harassing the enemy, and his methods won him respect from leaders in both the rebel and Royalist armies. He served the cause of freedom in Veracruz extremely well and before long the attempt to eliminate Victoria and his guerrilla tactics in the province of Veracruz caused it to become one of the principal theaters of war.

Victoria found the tropic areas served as excellent cover for his limited troops. He constructed small forts and fortified them with trusted followers. The men hit their projected targets of convoys, Royalist soldiers and mule trains, then melted into the forests or converged into their fortified and well-stocked hideouts. They gathered tolls from the merchants, demanded agricultural goods from the Spanish hacendados and sacked the surrounding countryside if sympathy was shown the Royalist troops.

In some cases many had come to fear the Royalist and rebel soldiers alike; but Guadalupe Victoria was known for his fairness and honesty and usually tried to repay those who extended him aid. Beltrami, who was in Mexico in the late 1820s said: "Victoria was a distinguished soldier and sincere patriot who played a natural part in the spirit of useful knowledge--fruit of his education in the College of San Ildefonso. He showed ambition, in spite of failure. Men of such character were not too easy to find in a nation that was composed mostly of Spaniards and Jesuit autocrats, and all the other debris of anarchy. Men who could raise above selfish motives, superstition and ignorance were few."[1]

Other insurgent leaders must have had the same feeling for the cause of freedom and independence as Victoria, but they were not as imaginative in their approach to their activities in the drastic and dramatic overtures as was Victoria. Few of them were as willing to accept adversities and sacrifice as was Victoria. Alamán in his history is very critical of all actions of this revolutionary leader; but Ramírez cites his nobility of character and the sincere religious beliefs which were the guiding characteristics of all of Victoria's activities. Ramírez justifies any imaginativeness on the part of Victoria in that all men who seek a better and more Utopian state are the dreamers, planners, and builders who carry through civilization the ideas that develop nations; and that the insurgent leader was such a man.[2]

The same philosophy holds in other earnest enterprises of Victoria. The royalist battle cry was: "¡Viva el Rey! ¡Viva nuestra Señora de los Remedios!"; whereas the counter-cry of the insurgents was "¡Viva la America! ¡Viva nuestra Señora de Guadalupe!" The Virgen de los Remedios was the honored religious banner

2. Virgen de los Remedios. Photograph reproduced from _México en seis siglos de evolucion_, with permission of the Mexican Consulate, Albuquerque, New Mexico.

3. Virgen de Guadalupe. Photograph reproduced from *México en seis siglos de evolucion*, with permission of the Mexican Consulate, Albuquerque, New Mexico.

of the conquistadors and the Spaniards, while that of the liberating army was the Virgen de la Guadalupe. It is little wonder that Victoria used his adopted name as a rallying cry, not for personal aggrandizement, but as a focal point of his strong religious beliefs and the desire for freedom for his native land.[3]

Alamán in his later years grudgingly recognized the ability of Victoria in battle and his successful exploits in Veracruz, which earned him the rank of Colonel. This recognition was bestowed upon him by Lic. Juan Nepemuceno Rosains for his effective harassment of the enemy, the delay of convoys traveling from the capital to Veracruz, and his capture of needed supplies from the Royalist munitions convoys.[4]

When Guadalupe Victoria first assumed command replacing Anaya, the men had joked about the weak appearance of this new leader; but he soon gained their respect by his firmness and honesty in the treatment of the troops and his ability to slash at the enemy's flanks and leave them crippled while the insurgents grabbed the prize of guns, supplies or expensive trade goods. For many months he worked with José Correa, a priest who had embraced the cause of independence with great enthusiasm under Hidalgo, and who--under Morelos --had been active in the Valladolid and Puruarán area before being transferred to the Veracruz province under Rosains in 1813. Correa reported in his memoirs that Victoria made his appointed rounds as a messenger, made useful contacts with all detachments, and that he had made friends with the _Jarochas_ (Negro troops) who fondly called him "Don Guadalupe" with great courtesy. Correa told of several expeditions and experiences with the _Jarochas_ in this fashion: "During our march we had a group of negroes who were absolutely insubordinate. However, we had the honor of having with us on this journey, going to Acasónica [in the jurisdiction of Huatusco] a modest young man with the title of Coronel --Don Félix Fernández [sic] who was filled with enthusiasm and had taken the pseudonym of Guadalupe Victoria, I, having the honor of standing in as godfather. . . . He was successful in making friends with all and soon earned their respect."[5]

Victoria appeared to be indefatigible, constantly on horseback, riding from one defense area to another. He slept in the countryside or in some hut of reeds, generally without many provisions except for some dry meat tied to the saddle or some tortillas carried in his supply bag. The young officer had all the attributes necessary for the life of a Mexican insurgent in the Veracruz province. His many successes and his popularity with the peasantry created a great reputation of competency and a myth of heroism that aroused jealousy in many of his fellow chiefs.

Victoria carried on the struggle for independence with diversionary tactics, always with valor and decisiveness in spite of the handicap of unsuitable weapons and little financial aid to obtain supplies. His forces generally amounted to about 2000 troops. Many times he attacked his foe even when outnumbered. He was always indomitable and tranquil in battle, ready to face any sacrifice or danger since he possessed an abundance of faith in his cause. He was the first to attack the enemy and the last to withdraw from the battleground.

He became well acclimated to and knowledgable of the terrain from the shores of Nautla to the barren hills of Perote; through the tropical zone between Veracruz and Puebla to the hills of Orizaba and Jalapa. Don Guadalupe and his men could march their way through thick forests, over the river crossings and mountains with their innumerable caves where shelter was always available. He often divided his forces into small groups, hit the convoys unexpectedly and carried off the cargoes he desired, or demanded a ransom for passage. At times this ransoming of cargoes could lead to problems for at one time Guadalupe Victoria harassed the group led by a Spanish merchant Don Miguel Menéndez who left Jalapa with mail, passengers and cargo expecting safe journey only to be delayed by the insurgent chief at Los Manatiales although he had paid ransom to Rosains. Many chieftains kept these funds for themselves and this created problems after Morelos's death and was one of the factors that led to the dissolution of the first Mexican congress.

Guadalupe Victoria was in many ways a benign warrior. He treated prisoners with respect, never torturing them or killing them cruelly as did some of the other chieftains. This is verified by the renowned Mexican historian, Francisco de Paula de Arrongoiz, who wrote rather disparagingly of Victoria, but who did admit that the insurgent leader was never a wanton killer. He says, "Although he was an understanding man, he was also careless, boastful and overly imaginative; but not a sanguinary killer as some of the other insurgents."[6]

Victoria and the other chieftains kept on creating havoc with the Royalist troops and convoys even though they appeared leaderless without Morelos or the congress. They retained control over the areas they had undertaken to defend. Mier y Terán retained his headquarters in Tehuacán; Sesma and Guerrero protected their interests in the South; while Osorno, Torres, Correa, Calzada, Rosales, Vargas and Rayón retained their independence and roamed various areas north of Mexico City.

These chieftains undertook little concerted action

but worked out their own logistics. Mier y Terán did attempt to bring all the leaders together and to set up a provisional executive committee, but few of the insurgent chiefs were interested and the plan was consequently abandoned and with this inaction vanished the representative government established by Morelos.[7]

Mier y Terán and Victoria did not cooperate too well after the former had ridiculed Victoria at Oaxaca. Had they gotten along, some of the early efforts of the insurgents might have been more successful instead of leading to defeat. Mier y Terán was not popular with Vicente Guerrero either, and with these two not caring about a triumvirate, the rest of the chieftains did not fall into line. Ramón Sesma, it may be recalled, was with Morelos at Oaxaca and had been responsible for the attack on the church and convent of La Soledad. José Francisco Osorno had joined the rebel forces in 1811. He had been a companion of Anaya and had spent much of his time against the Royalist armies in Veracruz, Tulancingo and Apam. Correa has been mentioned earlier as has Ignacio Rayón. José Antonio Torres had joined the revolution in 1810 and had spent most of his time in the area of Cóporo, El Sombrero and Los Remedios. The other chieftains were free-lancers who appeared to be more interested in personal gain than in winning independence for Mexico.

This lack of cooperative interest in a ruling body created a total disorganization of the independent forces. The Royalists were pleased by the discord among the insurgents; and they received more support from the Spaniards who saw a possible disintegration of the rebel movement. Some of the Criollos from whom the insurgents were stealing crops and supplies turned against the rebels, as many of these landlords were beginning to look upon them as ordinary bandits.

In the province of Veracruz, however, Guadalupe Victoria continued to receive support. His excellent knowledge of the terrain enabled him to utilize the dense woods with skill. Dealing a blow against the enemy in one area one day, he struck somewhere else the next. The Royalists were confused by his tactics and the convoys frequently fell into his hands, especially in the region of the Puente del Rey (now Puente Nacional). This famous bridge was on the main road to Mexico City via Jalapa and Orizaba along which most of the caravans from Veracruz had to pass. It was Guadalupe Victoria's favorite point of attack.[8]

The roads, rivers, and the overgrown jungle were such that a few men could attack a convoy, successfully carry away much bounty, and melt into the countryside. The area made the convoys vulnerable to attack by Victoria and his men who struck fast, grabbed the booty and retreated before they could be apprehended by the protecting Royalist troops.

Bancroft reports that in lieu of goods that "traders broke rules, purchased passes from the insurgents providing the latter with considerable revenue to sustain the war."[9] In many cases, the insurgents preferred to accept a ransom payment rather than to take the materials in the convoy, as some of the items were not always useful or a readily disposable product. The government was upset at these tactics and forbade the merchants to ransom their goods; but the directives were often ignored. Many times they would rather pay and pass in peace.

Occasionally after a severe skirmish it would be reported that Victoria had been injured or killed. There would be rejoicing in Mexico City that this scourge of the trail had been eliminated, only for the Spaniards to learn that Victoria had struck again. As Alperovich reports: "but to the end, some days this intrepid fighter, with his hat whirling like the wake of a ship, led his detachments around the enemy, subduing them and taking their cargoes."[10]

Upon Morelos's death Rosains had sought to take control of the various chieftains; however, they ignored his directives and went their own way, as was mentioned earlier. When Ignacio Rayón vacated Valladolid, discouraged by the progress of the Royalists and the childish antics of his compatriots, Rosains sent into the territory, Ramón Sesma. However, Morelos had originally assigned this territory to Vicente Guerrero; and when Sesma came on the scene, there was much tension and it appeared the leaders would begin to fight among themselves. Rosains eased the difficulty by assigning Guerrero to the Chilapa region with the rank of Colonel. Guerrero accepted and this move averted a conflict.

Rosains continued his manipulations in the Veracruz area and his activities were beginning to annoy other insurgents who were subject to him from the days he was appointed by Morelos. The climax came when Rosains sent a message to the Spanish in Veracruz offering security to the convoys of the Spanish merchants if they paid him a set levy. The other insurgents considered this a treasonable act and took action against him.[11]

Victoria was especially annoyed by this action as he had achieved good success with stopping convoys and extracting from them a levy or ransom in order to proceed, and the funds from this activity had financed his war effort.

Not being able to gain revenues for himself in the fashion described above, Rosains tried to get Osorno to accompany him in an attack on General Márquez Donallo, whose territory he wanted to annex. Osorno refused and stayed at the hacienda de Atlamajac, not realizing that Donallo had intercepted Rosains's

4. This sketch of Puente del Rey, now Puente Nacional, was made by Mrs. H. G. Ward, wife of the English Ambassador. It was found in H. G. Ward, History of Mexico (London: Henry Colburn, 1828).

messenger and learned about Rosains's plans. The general met the Rosains forces at Saltepec, near Huamantla, on January 22, 1815 and soundly defeated them.[12]

Rosains escaped Donallo's trap, but he became impotent because many of his troops left him to join Mier y Terán at Tehuacán and some joined Victoria. Rosains, annoyed at the other chiefs, began to attack those who had been his allies. The result was that Osorno, Arroya and Calzada declared their independence from Rosains and adhered to Victoria, choosing him as their lieutenant-general.[13]

Rosains, in his resentment, attacked some of the towns held by his former aides, but he was arrested by Mier y Terán who removed him from his command on August 20, 1815, sending him in chains from one chieftain to another. However, he managed to escape, accepted the indulto (pardon extended by the Virrey), and made many exposures of information of insurgent plans to the Royalist forces before retiring to Puebla.[14]

With the disposal of Rosains, the independents redivided their areas of activity with Osorno, assuming command of the flatlands of Apam, Victoria taking over

5. A current view of Puente del Rey, now Puente Nacional. Photo by the author.

the entire province of Veracruz, Mier y Terán remaining in Tehuacán and Mezteca, and Guerrero continuing his campaigns in the southern mountains. Other chiefs were scattered in the Chapala and Michoacán area. At this time the insurgents most active were: Mier y Terán with about 2000 followers, Victoria having the same, Osorno with less than 2000, with Ignacio Rayón having about 700 followers. Bravo and Galeana still had 800 followers, while Vicente Guerrero carried out his fight with 500 troops. The independent rebels in the Chapala area numbered about 700 with a large concentration in Michoacán of 4000. Rosales accounted for 300 men while free-lancers in the Bajio area claimed 800. The total complement of troops that the chieftains could dredge up totaled 13,800. These troops were in widely scattered areas, without any effective means of communication, poorly established discipline and without a governmental body that they could depend upon or be subject to for direction. Several attempts were made to set up juntas which would unify the chiefs, but they refused to recognize these. Consequently in the period from December 1815 until the middle of 1816 there was much confusion which led to a disinterest in keeping up the fight. The results were desertions, dissolving of organized units and finally capitulations because of the generosity of the pardons or indultos by Apodaca.[15]

Victoria was one of the few leaders who continued to harass the enemy. His major point of fortification and attack, as was mentioned earlier, remained at Puente del Rey. This important bridge over the Antigua River was a pass difficult to traverse and closed in with jungle on each side. Here he continued to disrupt communication and supply trains between Veracruz and Mexico City. His hit and run tactics continued to be effective with his small contingency of men attacking and retreating rapidly, harassing the troops, carrying off food, ammunition and animals, then immediately dispersing to a selected rendezvous. At this secluded place they gathered their stores and tended to the wounded. They would return, after a short span of rest, to continue their diversionary tactics even before the enemy troops could regather their stunned forces or fully realize the smallness in number of the rebel trrops which had attacked them.[16]

Ward gives this version of one incident: "Nor were Victoria's exploits confined to this desultory warfare. In 1815 he detained a convoy of 6000 mules escorted by 2000 men under the command of Colonel Aguila, at Puente del Rey (a pass, the natural strength of which the insurgents had fortified by placing artillery on its heights, by which it was commanded) nor did it reach Veracruz for upwards six months."[17]

Guadalupe Victoria was followed with enthusiasm by his troops and continued to be a real scourge to his enemies. However, the Spanish were determined to thwart him and in the latter months of 1815 imported from Spain additional troops led by Don Fernando Miyares, an excellent strategist, who with a contingency of 2000 troops was assigned to the province of Veracruz with but one purpose in mind--elimination of Victoria.

Victoria's troops were soon to feel the vengeance of the superior Royalist troops. Miyares began his tactics by establishing a chain of fortified posts on the entire road from Veracruz to Mexico City. While doing this he was given constant reinforcements and equipment. This enabled him to keep engaging Victoria's bands of men in constant action, which weakened the defenses of the insurgents, depleting the troops until they began to suffer major defeats. Gradually the rebel defenders were driven from the major stronghold of Puente del Rey and the lesser fortification at Puente San Juan.

The insurgent general's attempt to fight against these heavy odds proved fruitless. The constant battering by the Royalist troops, the superior equipment, regular supplies and rations of the opposition reduced the rebels to a ragged bunch of refugees. By the end of 1816 most of the original troops who had followed Don Guadalupe's leadership had fallen in battle.

When the new Viceroy, Juan Ruiz de Apodaca, formerly Capitan-General of Cuba, arrived in September 1816 with an additional 1000 troops, the situation became very grave, especially when the Virrey was authorized to extend the pardon or indulto to the rebel troops and to allow them liberal terms of amnesty if they were willing to give up their opposition to the Spanish government.

The five years of constant warfare had broken the spirit of many of the soldiers who had little respite from the constant fighting. They missed their homes, peace, and family and many readily accepted the indulto and returned to their homes. The replacements that Victoria could obtain were not the same caliber as that of the earlier patriots who had fought wholeheartedly for the cause of freedom. As the fervor of the natives decreased in the presence of the superior forces, the guerrillas faced defeat. They were not able to get food and arms freely. They were insufficiently clothed to combat the elements which could vary from the heat of the tropics to the freezing cold of the heights around Orizaba and Jalapa or the misty valleys between Jalapa and Perote. Ammunition was running low and fewer supplies were being obtained from their raids. The small amount of munitions that could be manufactured locally was not enough to distribute among the various leaders of the insurrection. The men began to desert in large numbers and before long General Guadalupe Victoria had fewer and fewer followers to carry on the running battle.

Priestley says of him: "Guadalupe Victoria . . . was a symbol of the hopelessness of the liberal cause, not less the symbol of its undying aspiration. Victory under the banner of the Virgin of Guadalupe, the sentiment of his ambition and of his romantic pseudonym was never to come to the liberal revolution."[18]

The guerrilla army was gradually being driven northward, where, after the loss of the major forts on the convoy trail, the only remaining fort or stronghold left was at Monte Blanco, which was on the road to Orizaba from which convoys swung to Puebla and Mexico City. Miyares had achieved his goal and now the main convoy route from Veracruz to Mexico City was functioning again without interference from the rebels.

The troops entrenched in the fort of Monte Blanco had withstood several minor assaults in October 1816, but the defending forces had dwindled to 250 men. Although the fort was strongly constructed, having been planned by Victoria under the direction of Coronel

Melchoir Múzquiz and his aide, Coronel Juan Mori, who were in charge of the area. A siege of eight days--in which supplies and water dwindled to nothing--made it necessary for the men to capitulate on November 7, 1816, to Coronel Márquez Donallo.

Some of the roving bands of Victoria's detachments had tried to stop the advances of the Royalists at Chocamán, but they were routed and dispersed by Donallo who had gone to Monte Blanco to aid José Iberri, who had been sent from Veracruz to help in clearing the last of the remnant rebels from the convoy trails. After Múzquiz surrendered his full complement of men to the Royalist forces, he was marched to Orizaba by the triumphant Donallo and was later imprisoned in Puebla.[19] He was pardoned in 1820 and retired to private life, not to reappear until the consummation of the independence in 1824.

After Victoria and his troops were driven from their strongholds along the trails to Mexico City, they moved near the coastal areas of Nautla and Boquilla de Piedras, where for a time he was able to obtain supplies from the United States and carry on his campaigns. Most of these goods came from New Orleans where José Joaquín de Herrera, as representative of the defunct rebel government, had gone to entice aid and munitions for the insurgents. Other representatives were still active in Washington, Philadelphia, and New York where they found many sympathetic supporters.[20]

In May 1816 the port of Boquilla de Piedras was visited by a ship under the direction of William Davis Robinson, a citizen of the United States. He had a cargo of 4000 muskets for Mier y Terán. Victoria presumably demanded an exhorbitant price to transmit the guns to Mier y Terán, and when refused payment, he did not allow the guns to be disembarked. A messenger was sent to Mier y Terán and a conference held between the two rebel leaders. They could not reach agreement on terms and although Guerrero was asked to intercede in the dispute, he refused. Frustrated by the delays, Robinson traveled to Tehuacán to make arrangements on a new delivery point. He and Mier y Terán were on their way to the port when they were attacked by Royalist troops.

Mier y Terán managed to escape, but Robinson, after eluding the enemy for five days, finally surrendered. He tried to talk his way out of his difficulties, but his captors thought they had landed the notorious revolutionary, Dr. John Robinson, and they kept William Davis Robinson under close surveillance first imprisoning him in Oaxaca, later transferring him to Veracruz and then to the Castillo de San Juan de Ulúa in the bay outside of the city. Finally he was sent to Spain where he managed to escape and returned to the United

States, later writing of his exploits in a book of Memoirs.[21]

Since it was apparent that Robinson was not going to return after an absence of several weeks, Victoria released the vessel and its cargo, and it returned to Galveston. It was this type of disunity among the chiefs, especially of Mier y Terán and Victoria, that was to prove fatal to the revolutionary movement. The growing reinforcements of the royalist troops--who with their superior equipment, supplies and munitions and their constant aggression--were able to break the will of the revolutionaries to continue their fight.

Resistance was at its lowest ebb, and more of the insurgents--leaders and troopers alike--began to take advantage of the indulto offered. Victoria was forced to retreat constantly. It was a trying period for all who had fought so diligently and so long for independence, yet were unable to attain their goal. Victoria was determined not to surrender, nor to accept the pardon so generously offered with many favorable terms.

Robinson, who had felt that Guadalupe Victoria was somewhat responsible for his imprisonment in Mexico and Spain, still admired the tenacity of Victoria to the republican cause. In his memoirs he wrote the following: "More than twenty times the Mexican Gazette has published that Victoria was slain, and his party annihilated; but a few days after those false and pompous accounts, we have heard of Victoria suddenly springing up, attacking and capturing convoys of merchandise, seizing some stronghold, and throwing the whole country in consternation. At the head of one hundred to two hundred cavalry, he performed some of the most daring exploits that were effected during the revolution; and his personal courage and activity were universally acknowledged, even by his enemies. More than four-fifths of the population of Vera Cruz were in his favor."[22]

Victoria's forces in the north near Nautla and Boquilla de Piedras had been pummelled for months. With the fall of Monte Blanco in November 1816, the Royalist forces controlled the area from Orizaba northward and eastward toward the coast. They began to move toward the forts north of Veracruz. The governor of Veracruz, Don José Dávila, ordered Coronel José Antonio Rincón into the area with some of his artillerymen. The insurgents offered strong opposition, but the death in battle of Victoria's trusted leader, Don José María Villapinto, resulted in the loss of the area and the disintegration of the remainder of Victoria's followers and the complete destruction of the coastal supply lines.

Throughout the Veracruz province the trap was closing in. The men began to desert the cause of independence, especially when the villages that supplied the insurgent general were being destroyed by the Royalists and the inhabitants' possessions and lands devastated. Contributions of any type were slow in coming and in some areas were nonexistent. The Virrey Apodaca offered Guadalupe Victoria the indulto, which he again refused. Mayer states that the Virrey made "efforts to seduce Victoria from his principles and to ensure his loyalty; but he refused rank and rewards offered by the Viceroy as the price of submission."[23]

Ellis P. Bean, an American participant in the Mexican War for independence, had been with the Galeanas at Cuautla Ampilas in 1812 and had fought against the Calleja army. He had become acquainted with Victoria and had some contact with him on several occasions. He mentions in his diary:

> Morelos had been taken by the Royalists and shot. . . . I went to Tehuacán. . . . There I learned that Colonel Muscos was taken to Palo Blanco near Huatusco. I returned to the latter place where I had about $1400. I packed it up and started to meet General Victoria, who had gone down the coast, a small distance from Vera Cruz. I took with me a young lady of fine family who had lost all they had in the revolution. [Señorita Anna Garthas, a relative of the deceased Morelos.] I married her. . . . I stopped at a hacienda. The next day General Victoria came on, having with him but four men. He had been beaten by the Royalists and was then on his retreat. He was entirely destitute of funds. I told him what I had proposed that we should unite and make a new effort. He said it was not worthwhile, that the people had got out of heart, and it would be better to go to some secret place and there wait till there was a change. He wanted me to join him; but I could not think of hiding myself; besides the very men who would bring me provisions, would betray me into the hands of the enemy. I told him I would send my wife to Jalapa, and make my way to the United States by land if it took me two years. General Victoria said it was impossible for him to do it. The next morning he left me and went into the mountains, not far from Córdoba where he remained, living the life of a hermit.[24]

Victoria sought refuge at Palmillas for a while and later stayed at the Hacienda de Paso de Ovejas; but he was driven out again and hounded by the Spanish troops, this time led by Commander José Trevasi, who was sent out from Puebla to pursue the insurgent general.[25]

While Victoria was being sought in all the reaches

of the Veracruz province, another drama that would have little effect upon him, but added to the disaster of the fight for Mexican independence, was taking place in England in the early months of 1816. There the tempestuous Fray Servando Teresa de Mier Noriega y Guerra was seeking persons to aid the Mexicans in their struggle. The Fray contacted a young Spanish patriot who had sustained a brilliant career in Spain fighting against the French invaders of that country. His career in Spain almost paralleled that of Victoria in the province of Veracruz. This Spanish patriot, Javier Mina y Larrea, was the same age as Victoria and had spent most of his youth fighting against Napoleonic forces and later those of Ferdinand VII after the abolishment of the provisional constitutional government. He had to flee for his life and ended up as an exile in England. Fray Mier persuaded him to undertake the cause of Mexican independence; and Mina left Liverpool on the fifth of May, 1816 with a small group of mercenaries, arriving in Baltimore on July 3, 1816.

While in the United States, Mina and Mier were able to persuade others to give them financial support and by the end of August had been able to recruit 200 men and a ship. Mina sailed to Santo Domingo on his way to his rendevous at Galveston where he would pick up directions and supplies. Here he encountered a lengthy delay because of the attempts by Spanish officials, especially the Spanish Minister, Don Luis de Onís, to stop the expedition. However, Onís could not stop the journey and Mina finally sailed from Galveston in early May, 1817 after having had many problems with illness and desertion which took toll of his small group of volunteers.

Fray Mier had gone ahead of Mina's expedition to make contact with Guadalupe Victoria, who had been holding the ports of Boquilla de Piedras and Nautla. Mier did not know of the disastrous results of the rebel armies in the northern part of Veracruz and when he arrived at the coastal landings and learned of the retreat of Victoria and his inability to contact him, he returned to Galveston. However, due to a severe storm he arrived in that city too late to warn Mina. Therefore, Mina was unaware that the rebel armies were on the wane and that the majority of the independent troops were either deserting or taking the *indulto*.

Fate, indeed in its whimsy, plays many tricks and this was a most tragic one, for Mina's subsequent landing at Soto la Marina had little support. Most of the remaining forces fighting for independence were chiefly in the central and southern provinces around Guanajuato, El Sombrero, Los Remedios and Michoacán. These troops had their own problems and were not free to come to Mina's aid even if they had been aware of him. As soon as Mina's troops landed on the twenty-first of April there was some dissension due to the lack of support that had been anticipated. The Spanish dispersed a sizeable amount of troops against the invaders. Mina managed to get as far as El Sombrero when he was opposed by the forces of Colonel Liñan. In his retreat, which occupied the better part of several months, Mina and his cohorts were driven from the area and made a final stand near Orrantia at the ranch of El Vanadito where Mina was captured by Liñan, condemned to death and shot on November 11, 1817. So ended another episode of the ironic circumstances that subdued the interest in the war against Spain. The patriots became more fearful of extending aid to anyone, including the hard-pressed insurgents. The American privateers and others interested in aiding the Mexicans to attain their freedom, seeing the gradual defeat of the rebels and not receiving their payments for the supplies being sent, decreased their support, and the cause of the freedom for the Mexicans began to wane rapidly.

Miguel i. Vergés puts it very poignantly: "The Grito de Dolores had its last agonizing pangs with Mina in Cerro de Ballaca in 1817."[26] As for Victoria, the fugitive general was aided by the peons in the foothills of Orizaba for a short time; but the burning of the villages and crops by the Royalist troops and the constant harassment of the people who had sympathized and aided the revolutionary leaders jeopardized the lives of all. These people--fearing the wrath and harsh retaliation of the Spanish troops--refused to aid all leaders, including Victoria. The General, realizing the despair and fear of his supporters, retreated farther into the jungle of Veracruz. In this way it did stop some of the sufferings of his people. He disappeared completely in the middle of the year 1818, not to be heard from for over two and one-half years.[27]

Viceroy Apodaca--fearing that General Victoria, a favorite of the masses, might still find some support for his activities--resorted to placing a price on the capture or death of Victoria. The Viceroy sent out Brigadier Llano, Commandante General of Puebla to ferret out the rebel leader. Llano transferred the responsibility for Victoria's manhunt to his son-in-law, Don José Barradas, and gave him a force of men to seek him out. In turn Barradas communicated with Rafael Pozos, who had been a sergeant-major in the insurgent forces and had taken the indulto in 1818. He persuaded Pozos to contact a captain of Victoria's troop, Valentín Guzmán, to betray the General or convince him to surrender. The ruse was not successful.

The search for Victoria continued unabated for about six months, but fortunately he was able to evade his pursuers. At times he was near enough to hear the soldiers curse both Apodaca and himself: Apodaca for causing the soldiers to patrol the fetid undergrowth of the jungle and Victoria for his elusiveness. Finally the hunt for the fugitive insurgent was abandoned after reports of finding the decomposed remains were circulated and officially published in the Gazette de Mexico [sic].[28]

Victoria was to roam over the province of Veracruz for thirty months. The sufferings he underwent were severe. In some areas his body was slashed by the thorny undergrowth which rendered his clothes to rags and cut his flesh. The cuts on his festering body were aggravated by swarming insects. Food scarcity was especially acute in winter, and he was often without nourishment, though in the summertime the harvesting of wild fruit sustained his needs. However, the lack of a sufficiency of food weakened him and at times made him faint.

The area in which Victoria roamed ranged from the snow-capped mountain of Orizaba to the dry plateau area near Perote. In between was the fetid tropic area that led to the ocean and to the port of Veracruz. Victoria seldom went far from this area as he knew how dangerous it was to approach the shorelines or waters near Nautla or Boquilla de Piedras. He spoke of his experiences to a few intimates but never went into any great detail about his hiding places although Ward affirms the general repeatedly told him: ". . . No repast had afforded him as great a pleasure as when, after being without food for some time, he was able to gnaw the bones of dead animals which he found in the woods."[29]

With the disappearance of Victoria into the fastness of the Orizaba region, it appeared that most of the dissent in the province of Veracruz was ended. Mariano Cuevas says of this time: "The troops were diminished by annihilation, desertions, natural disheartening and capitulations. Such were the consequences, as much as the capitulations, which brought about the condition that led to the persecutions of the old insurgents."[30]

There is little question that Apodaca's less sanguinary attitude and extensive use of the indulto did much to lead to the loss of strength of the leaders of the revolution. When a few of the patriots turned to outright banditry, even the most sincere of the supporters among the Criollos turned to Spanish support to overcome the resulting anarchy and despotism. The light of victory for Mexican independence was well on the way to being extinguished completely.

From the extensive diaries that Apodaca left, it is apparent that the indulto with its generous terms and rewards led to the retirement of many of the rebel chieftains and their followers. Some even joined the ranks of the Spanish army and had great influence on the outcome of the revolution by betraying the outposts and plans of the few surviving fighters.[31]

Another factor was the rape of the land, the crops and the wealth of the supporters of the revolution. Most of the valuables of the hacendado were gone, trade was reduced to nothing. The mines had fallen into disuse since few could be found to labor in them. Few vessels entered the boycotted ports. Smuggling by American privateers and entrepreneurs was no longer profitable for there was no guarantee of payment for supplies of arms and ammunition or other trade goods. For many years after the establishment of the Mexican republic there would be suits for recovery of funds invested by these persons in pursuit of freedom by Mexican revolutionists.

The favorable balance of trade was now with the victorious army. With Guadalupe Victoria out of the picture and the strength of the patrolling Royalist armies predominant, the province of Veracruz was at peace for the first time since 1810. The vigilance of the Pascual Mariscal del Campo Liñan's forces along the convoy trails--which had been first secured by Miyares --meant that for the first time in a decade convoys were able to proceed in comparative safety, hindered infrequently by danger of attack, except for an occasional group of ineffectual brigands.

Bancroft, in discussing the last days of this sad period in Mexican history, states the facts in this way:

> The revolution in its first period had terminated. The efforts of Hidalgo, Morelos, Bravos and others apparently had been in vain. The sacrifice of blood and treasure, the heroic sufferings, the great examples of pure and exalted character and high courage, the prowess of men like Victoria, Matamoros, Trujano, Galeana, Mina and others had availed nought . . . and this result was due mainly to the absence of union among a number of prominent chiefs, to rivalries and jealousies on the part of others . . . and to the lack of discipline shown by many leaders. . . ."[32]

There appears to be little doubt that if some of the chieftains such as Mier y Terán, Osorno, Rayón, Guerrero and Victoria had been able to cooperate more closely and "forgive and forget" their personal differences, the struggle for independence might have come to a fortuitous end, despite the loss of Morelos who had welded these men together into an effective fighting unit.

Many persons in Spain and Mexico hailed Virrey

Apodaca as a man of peace. However, there were still a few who issued pamphlets, newspapers and handbills against his regime. These were very critical of his rule and they castigated him for being intolerant of freedom of the press, an instigator of disunity, power hungry and a pawn of indiscreet politicians. These men, it was said, sought power and wealth and had little love for any kind of freedom for New Spain as it would cut into their personal gains and restrict their opportunities.

Numerous articles and pamphlets contained poetic doggerel of which the following is a sample:

> Si un Virey es persona de
> autoridad superior.
> Será licito tratarlo
> con infamia, y deshonor?[33]

However, the peace was not to last, for circumstances in Spain would be such that the Mexican patriots would again be striving for a more personal voice in the government and would seek self-recognition for their nation. Strangely enough, the changes would be sought from the army and clergy which had striven so hard to overcome the original cry for independence of the Mexican nation from Spanish domination.

The change was brought about when military leaders in Spain revolted and restored in March 1820, the Constitution of 1812. They compelled the King, Ferdinand VII, to accept and to support it. When the news reached Mexico in April 1820, some of the Spaniards were in support of it, while others were fearful of it, feeling that the liberals in Spain would pass laws liberalizing the rights of the Mexican populace and in this fashion reduce the power of those in public office and lessening the hold of the church leaders over the people. The effects could be disastrous, according to the beliefs of the conservatives. These people, who were responsible for the long siege and sanguinary warfare for ten long years, were the same group who for their own selfish interests now planned to revive the battle and to seek ways of turning the advantages of any type of constitutional reform to their continuance in power, for to lose control of the current situation meant expulsion from the country, loss of public office, confiscation of church property and anonymity.

6. The governors of Mexico at the time of the Revolution. Photograph reproduced from México en seis siglos de evolucion with permission of the Mexican Consulate, Albuquerque, New Mexico.

CHAPTER FOUR

FROM IMPERIALISM TO INDEPENDENCE:

1821-1824

For thirty months Guadalupe Victoria roamed the foothills and jungles of Veracruz as a hermit. His was an existence of complete isolation. Various of his detractors ridiculed his stories in later life, but truth has its way of sometimes making fiction appear ridiculous. He had many sympathetic listeners and among them in the early 1820s was the English traveler, W. B. Bullock. A vivid account of one of the General's experiences is related by Bullock as follows:

> His privations and sufferings during that period almost exceed credibility. His precarious existence depended on vegetables and insects, procured in the forests where he resided, without the smallest communication with his fellow creatures. At one time, in consequence of his mental and corporeal sufferings, he was attacked by a fever and remained for eleven days at the entrance of a cavern, stretched on the ground without food, hourly expecting termination of his wretched existence; so near death that vultures were constantly hovering over him in expectation of their prey. The first nourishment he received was the warm blood of one of these birds, which had approached to feast on his half-closed eyes, when he seized him by the neck and was by this means enabled to crawl to the nearest water to slake his parching thirst.[1]

One cannot help but wonder at this tale; but it is true that men in forests, deserts, and other outlandish circumstances have survived under many odd experiences. The time element might have been exaggerated, but it is true that Victoria had been given up for lost and that he did return to civilization under unusual privation.

At the time of his self-imposed exile, Guadalupe Victoria did not know of the political intrigues which would soon involve him in the beginning of a new revolution and that the destiny of Mexico would involve him again in the role of a freedom fighter for the independence of his beloved country. It had seemed prophetic that he had told Ellis Bean the time for the insurgents to take to the field again was on the horizon.

In January, 1820 the Rebellion of Riego in Spain forced Ferdinand VII to re-acknowledge the defunct Constitution of 1812. On March 9, 1820 the Spanish king announced the official acceptance of the Constitution and stated that it should be proclaimed to all the colonies.

When the Governor of Veracruz, José Dávila, received the official notification of the reinstatement of the Constitution of 1812, he told the gathering of landlords and merchants in the city of Veracruz that this day, March 25, 1820 would be a fateful one for Mexico. He said: "Gentlemen, you have asked me to carry through my obligation to proclaim and to swear to the Constitution; this will give hope to the independence, which is going to be the result of this."[2]

Shortly after the announcement was read in Mexico City in April 1820 by Apodaca, it stirred much unrest among the Spanish leaders. A group of leading clergymen, military officers led by Pedro Celestino Negrete, and many conservatives including the hacendados, merchants and public officials began to meet in secret in the rooms of the Church, La Profesa. They were worried about the liberal provisions in the Constitution which would limit the power of the Church, eliminate the Inquisition, oust present office holders from their lucrative positions and in other ways curb their power. It was rather ironic that this group, which had so strongly opposed the insurgent movement for self-government and caused its demise was now cast in the role of the fighters for freedom and the defenders of independence for Mexico, the same ideology which they had so strongly opposed for a decade.

Even more peculiar was the choice of leadership of the new independence group, the former Royalist army leader of Criollo descent, Agustín de Iturbide y Aramuburu. Iturbide's father was a native Spaniard from the province of Pamplona; but his mother was a native Mexican from an old family in Valladolid. He had joined the army and married the same year, when he was twenty-two years old. He appeared to be a liberal; but when he was approached to join Hidalgo's cause in 1810, he refused and became very devoted to his service to the Royalists.

Many times during his persistent fights against the independents he referred to them as perverts, bandits, and sacrilegious peasants. He had little mercy with them and was one of the most sanguinary of the Royalists. He had been commander in the Bajío region, but disliked that area and especially the area occupied by Vicente Guerrero. However, he had been involved in some extortion scandals and had been accused of unnecessary violence in dealing with his troops and the populace and had been removed from office by Apodaca. However, he had always been a staunch friend of the Church and many of the chief ecclesiasts supported him even after his retirement from the army.

There was some opposition to choosing Iturbide, but there were few others that they felt they could trust. They really had little choice, and Iturbide was a favorite of the clergy who attended the meetings. He was also considered a strong supporter of the monarchy and it was believed he would set up a government that would have influence with the royal family. With these plans of revolt approved, the next step was to obtain reinstatement of Iturbide in the army.

Influential people approached Viceroy Apodaca and prevailed upon him to give Iturbide the command post held by General D. H. Armijo, who was a firm believer in the Constitution. By getting rid of Armijo the conspirators hoped to weaken the supporters of the Constitution. These persons used the excuse that Iturbide was more capable of overcoming and subjugating the insurgent general, Vicente Guerrero, whose influence was still strong in southern Mexico.

Apodaca, surprisingly enough, readily acceded to this request and did reinstate Iturbide. It is assumed by some historians that the Virrey was actually part of a plot to discredit the establishment of the Constitution and wanted to retain Mexico under the power of Ferdinand VII.[3] Within a matter of days Iturbide began to build up and equip a sizeable force. He was confident that he could first defeat Guerrero, proclaim himself the head of the territory, then take steps to overcome the current government and establish himself as the ruler of Mexico. He was careful not to reveal his ambitions to his supporters at this time, but he awaited an opportune time to plan his coup.[4]

By the middle of November he was on his way south, and carried in his possession a shipment of gold which was to be sent to Spain from Acapulco. However, along the way he took into his confidence several of his senior officers whom he felt he could trust. Swearing them to secrecy he told them of his plan to dupe the conservatives in order to obtain more men and arms and then to make his declaration of independence from Spain. It was his intention, however, to make a good impresssion by overcoming Guerrero first as this would make him appear to be quite a heroic figure. Among his chief supporters were the Criollos, Coronel Pedro Celestino Negrete and José Mariano Michelena, who were to figure prominently in the new revolution. They aided him in building up the forces he needed and obtained for him a printing press, which was vital at this time for issuance of proclamations and other propaganda.

However, when Iturbide did make his stab at conquering Vicente Guerrero he was soundly trounced and was stalemated in every move he made to overcome the wily insurgent chief. In desperation at seeing his plans thwarted and his power fading away, Iturbide appropriated the 550,000 pesos in bullion he was carrying, printed a manifest which he wrote and proclaimed freedom for Mexico under the Plan of Iguala or the Plan of the Three Guarantees. The three guarantees were: national independence, the Catholic faith as the only faith, and equality and union of all classes.[5]

There were other articles in the Plan including means of setting up a monarchy, layout of duties of the Junta and a regency to be established. Other items included duties of a Congress to be organized, military regulations, and the use of the Spanish Constitution until new laws could be formed. The ambitions of Iturbide were great and he had little time in planning to take over supreme power. But, in order to do this, he realized that he had to win general support. Consequently, one of his first moves was to send a copy of the proclamation to Guerrero attempting to gain his support. The Plan did not mollify Guerrero, who had little liking or respect for Iturbide. However, Iturbide sent out other copies to Nicolás Bravo and several of the chiefs who had taken the indulto. Bravo accepted the terms of the Plan and was given the rank of coronel and agreed to participate in the new unification proposals. Trusting the judgment of his former associate, Vicente Guerrero accepted the terms and the new revolutionary movement was under way. By the end of February 1821 the proclamation was widely distributed and on March 2, 1821 was nationally proclaimed.

The Virrey, Juan Ruiz Apodaca, was invited to participate in the new revolution, but he refused to condone the situation and commanded the Royalist troops to take the field against the usurper, Iturbide. They refused to do so and joined the army of liberation. Virrey Apodaca was deposed by the Mariscales Liñan and Francisco Novella on July 5, 1821.

Apodaca left the following day with his family for the country resort at the Villa de Guadalupe, but the rebel army leaders requested that he return with his family to the Convento de San Fernando in Mexico City where he could be kept under surveillance. Here he and his family remained until September 24, 1821 when he was allowed to leave for Veracruz and embarked on the ship "Asia" to return to Spain.[6]

In March 1821 the province of Veracruz accepted Iturbide's leadership, with the exception of the port of Veracruz where Santa Anna had not been able to convince the Commandante José Dávila to give up his Royalist authority. In succeeding months the cities of

Valladolid and Querétaro fell to the combined forces of the liberation army. Many other cities surrendered without resistance: Don Antonío Leon took Oaxaca and Don José Joaquin de Herrera, who had played an important part in the United States in obtaining aid and supplies from various parties, took over Córdoba. Apatzingán was taken by Don Juan Domínguez and Coronel Don Miguel Barragán who had announced the Plan at the Villa de Tusantla.

As soon as the Plan of Iguala became known in the province of Veracruz, two faithful Indian followers of General Victoria set out to find the insurgent leader in the wilderness and to communicate to him the new occurrences. They sought for the self-exiled rebel leader for six weeks; and they were about to relinquish the search, believing that the General had indeed died during his exile. As they were leaving, one of them noticed a footprint in the sand of a ravine which they were crossing. Examining the footprint closely, one of the Indians recognized it as that of a white man because of the peculiar marking caused by a person having once worn shoes.

Knowing that a further search might prove futile, since they were short of rations, one of the Indians decided to attract the attention of the owner of the strange footprint by suspending some tortillas in the forested area near the ravine. He thought this unusual sign of human habitation might intrigue the person hiding in the area and keep him in the vicinity. The Indians then returned to a nearby village for supplies in order to continue the search. This crude plan was successful, as several days later Guadalupe Victoria, traversing the ravine, spied the food suspended in the tree and hungrily stuffed it into his mouth. It was his first taste of civilized food in thirty months, and he gave little immediate thought to the source of the food.

After gorging himself he began to reflect on the origin of the tortillas. He wondered whether friend or foe had left the provisions. Assuming that the person would return, Victoria lay in a safe ambush for several days to await the revelation as to whom the benefactors might be. His careful vigil was rewarded, for upon the return of the natives, he recognized one of them as a faithful follower. He rushed out precipitously to greet his rescuers, but they--upon seeing this apparition running toward them brandishing a sword--fled in terror.

Stopping only after hearing his name repeated several times, one of the Indians allowed the awesome figure, clad only in an old wrapper, to approach him. As Arenas said: "Indeed, Victoria was unrecognizable. His beard and hair had grown unbelievably long during this time; his nails had changed his hands to claws, his half-naked body was covered by a tattered blanket and he was emaciated and thin.[7]

This apparition, or phantom-like figure, of the former insurgent leader must have presented a sad spectacle to his rescuers. However, after some discussion and distribution of food to the starved revolutionary, the group departed to the nearest village, where the General was enthusiastically welcomed by all the villagers. The report of Victoria's miraculous reappearance spread rapidly throughout the province of Veracruz; and although at first not credited, the fact was received with enthusiasm when the insurgent leader appeared publicly. Many of his former followers flocked around him and rallied to the cause of the new independence movement when he declared his intention to join the cause.

On April 21, 1821 Guadalupe Victoria appeared at Santa Fe, a village near Veracruz, and issued a proclamation which told of his privations and sufferings for independence. He appealed to the people to unite themselves, end all war and establish a free Mexico. He ended his impassioned plea with the cry: "Dios, Independencia and Libertad."[8]

From the Campo de Santa Fe, Victoria went to seek Iturbide. On his way he allied himself with Nicolás Bravo at Tulancingo. They, in turn, formed a battalion with Herrera and laid siege to Puebla which held firm. However, Iturbide brought in additional forces after conquering Cuernavaca, and, after a discussion with General Llano, the city capitulated on August 2, 1821. Shortly thereafter, the major cities of Mexico, including Monterrey, Durango, Guadalajara, and Oaxaca, fell into the hands of the Army of the Three Guarantees.

Meanwhile on July 30, 1821 there had arrived in Veracruz a new Virrey, General Don Juan O'Donojú. The Captain-general of New Spain entered the country he was to rule unaware of the loss of Spanish control over Mexico. He learned that Veracruz, Acapulco, the Fortaleza de San Carlos at Perote and Mexico City were all that remained under Spanish domination.

O'Donojú, when approached by Iturbide at Córdoba, to which he had been escorted by Santa Anna, had little recourse except to agree to the terms laid out by Iturbide, and he signed the Treaty of Córdoba. The document essentially conserved the *Plan of Iguala*, but it guaranteed to the King of Spain the right to rule over Mexico as the emperor, or agreed to the assignment of another ruler of the Spanish family at the discretion of the Cortes, but guaranteed constitutional rule to the people of Mexico. The influence of the Constitution of 1812 was evident in the codification of the *Plan of Iguala* and the Treaty of Córdoba inasmuch as they recognized the rights of the individual, the protection of civil liberties by the government, and the personal liberties of the individual. Other concessions included the rights of the inhabitants of Mexico to representation in the Cortes, abolition of talks on embargo of cargoes from the Indies, and the suppression of the Inquisition.

Shortly after the agreement with O'Donojú, when the control of the army was fully in Iturbide's hands, Victoria came to Iturbide to offer his full cooperation and services. Iturbide arrogantly rejected the insurgent general's cooperation, implying he had no office or duty open to Victoria which he could fulfill. Iturbide realized that the rebel leader would not be a controllable puppet--as Victòria held rigid beliefs in the cause of freedom and independence for Mexico; and that some of Iturbide's ambitions might be thwarted by Victoria. The remark that presumably angered Victoria was the statement attributed to Iturbide in which he alluded to Victoria's activities in Oaxaca in 1812: "Si con atolito vamos sanando, atolito vámosle dando." ("You can fall into the mire and recover; but we might fall into the mire and be harmed.")[9]

Some writers ascribe Iturbide's sarcastic attitude toward Victoria to the fact that Victoria had presented to Iturbide a plan for a monarchy, the basis of which was that the monarch should be a Mexican, and that he should marry an Indian maiden to be named Malinche, alluding to the famous Doña María de Hernán Cortés. Iturbide considered this plan ridiculous. Zavala contends that Victoria had never made this statement, while Cuevas maintains that the statement is true as Iturbide wrote about this proposal to Negrete. However, no document providing these allegations has ever been found or verified.[10]

The implications in all this talk was, of course, that Victoria wanted to be the ruler since he had carried on the battle for independence while most of the current leaders had been on the other side of the conflict while he had worked hard for Mexican independence. Knowing the popularity of Victoria, it has been presumed that this propaganda was started to negate the importance of the insurgent leader and imply that the days in the jungle had perhaps affected his mind. However, though unhappy with the attitude of Iturbide, Victoria did encourage the people to fight for liberty and independence for Mexico and cooperated to attain that goal.

All the terms of the two treaties mentioned earlier were not satisfactory to all parties involved. Victoria was not the only person who was dissatisfied with some of the terms outlined. Many Criollo army officers who had remained loyal to Spain felt that they were being left out wrongfully and not being adequately recompensed for their loyalty.

During the war of independence, the Criollo troops proved to be the mainstay of the Spanish government. However, few of the Criollos had held any major commands and many of them saw the error of their ways when the Spanish predominance was again in the ascendency during 1818-1820. During the indulto period, crowds of insurgents were allowed to join the Royalist armies as recruits. They spread their doctrine of independence; and when Apodaca appeared hesitant in accepting the renewed Constitution of 1812, many of them were ready again to accept the independence of Mexico with themselves as the leaders of the army while the Criollo officers who had been loyal were apparently going to be left out of the sphere of influence. One of these was Don Antonio López de Santa Anna of whom we shall learn more shortly.

While the various leaders of the new revolution were trying to settle their differences, negotiations were still continuing with O'Donojú. Naturally, since most of the cities of Mexico were under rebel domination and his few troops were under siege in the few remaining cities loyal to the crown, there was little military support for him to summon and to try to overcome the rebellion, so he had made the best of the bargain. Hall says that "O'Donojú saw Mexico irretrievably lost on the terms, at least, in which it had been held heretofore. He endeavored to make the best conditions he could for his country."[11]

He did gain concessions in that he was able to retain some rights for the Spanish throne and for the Spaniards in Mexico. However, several of the Spanish officers resolved not to lay down their arms, but after some consultation with the Virrey, they did surrender rather reluctantly; and Acapulco, Veracruz province and Fortaleza de San Carlos at Perote capitulated. Mariscal Francisco Novello refused to surrender Mexico City and prepared to defend it. It was not until he received a stiff reprimand from O'Donojú, who reminded him that he was still the official representative from Spain, that he capitulated and surrendered his command.

Commander José Dávila, the governor of Veracruz, withdrew his command from the city of Veracruz and retreated to the Castillo San Juan de Ulúa, where he held the entry key to the harbor of Veracruz for Spain and created a serious problem for the Mexicans for several more years, before they finally liberated the bay.

The deposed Viceroy O'Donojú was escorted into Mexico City on September 25, 1821. Mariscal Francisco Novello turned over the command of the city to him and withdrew. The following day the Army of the Three

Guarantees marched into Mexico City led by Iturbide with a force of 16,000 troops which gave military assurance to the independence.

The Junta Provisional de Gobierno was installed by O'Donojú on September 28, 1821 and the act of independence as an established fact was set after a decade of deadly conflict. Ten days later O'Donojú was stricken with pleurisy and died. He was buried with honors in the nave of the Altar of Kings in the Cathedral of Mexico. Perhaps it was a restful end as subsequent results might have caused him to be imprisoned as a traitor to Spain had he tried to return to his native land.

The ruling Junta now consisted of the regency of Agustín Iturbide as president, assisted by Don Manuel de la Bárcena, Don Antonio Joaquín Peréz Martínez (replacing O'Donojú), Don Isidoro Yáñez, and Don Manuel Velásquez de León.[12] Later substitutions were Nicolás Bravo, Manuel de Heras Soto and Miguel Valentín for Bárcena and Velásquez de León.[13]

The victory of the three guarantees did create some major problems. One of them was the sudden exodus of many of the Spanish merchant/capitalists and public officials who were panicky about what might happen to them if they remained. They were very concerned about the rising power of the Criollos. The Spanish were allowed to leave without undue confiscation of property. Basil Hall says of this time: "The Mexican Cortes or Sovereign Constituent Congress finally met on February 24, 1822; and one of their first, if not the very first act, was an edict, permitting all who chose it to leave the country, and allowing them the export of specie at a duty of only three and one-half percent."[14]

The exodus of Spanish power and authority was helpful to the new class which was seeking control, and as Alperovich writes: "In some cases, where vacancies occurred, this permitted the high-ranking Criollos to strengthen their positions in the economy, the administration, the executive authority, the church and other sectors and correlation of the power of this group was reflected in the political structures which followed the proclamation of independence. . . ."[15]

However, in many ways this was an over-optimistic note as the exodus was detrimental to the government and the finances--as it left men without experience in all areas to take over the destiny of a new nation that was on the verge of bankruptcy--since most of the moneyed class had left the country and those now in power had little experience with the vicissitudes of international, local politics or economics; or the greed of men who for the first time have control over positions of power and money.

Attention was now concentrated upon plans to

establish a form of government. Iturbide proposed that two chambers should be constituted: one composed of twelve to fifteen clergymen, equal numbers of army officers, and one member from the major cities of the country; and a second to consist of deputies elected by the people based on one representative for every fifty thousand inhabitants.

The original concept was not acceptable to many of the leaders; but a compromise was worked out. The clause regarding the division by population was reserved; and it was directed that those provinces which elected more than four members should send one clergyman, one military man and a lawyer so that all classes might have representation. It was compulsory for the provinces to select representatives from among the agricultural, mining, commercial and artisan groups as well as the elite named above.

The liberals felt that this method of selection would still give most of the representation to the clergy and army, and they objected. The result was chaos and a great deal of dissension among the deputies attempting to set up a workable government to rule the new nation.

Furthermore, Iturbide's continuing arrogance, caprice and extravagances were appalling to the financially stricken nation's leaders. His handling of the Congress, by usurping their powers, alienated many of them. The deputies began to oppose him, especially Fray Servando Teresa de Mier Noriega y Guerra, Carlos María de Bustamante and Victoria. Others joined Victoria in a plot against Iturbide, using the home of Miguel Domínguez, former corregidor of Querétaro, as their headquarters. The plot against the government of Iturbide was betrayed by General Pedro Celestino Negrete, who was known to have liberal views and had been invited to join in the campaign to oust Iturbide as President of the Congress. Iturbide had the conspirators jailed on November 27, 1821. The culprits arrested included Don Nicolás Bravo, Coronel Arechavala, Brigadier Miguel Barragán, Guadalupe Victoria, Juan Morales (editor of several liberal publications), and others totaling seventeen in all.

They were formally accused of conspiring against the Plan of Iguala and the government, and plotting personal harm against Iturbide. After some time in prison and a stiff reprimand, all of the conspirators were released with the exception of Victoria and Morales. Victoria was incarcerated in the jail of the Palacio Nacional.

Bustamante was retained by Victoria as his attorney, and he was planning a plea before the legislature on the basis of illegal curtailment of the duties of a deputy (Victoria had been named a deputy from Durango), when the insurgent general was smuggled from the prison by Dr. Manuel Codorniu y Ferreras, Don Manuel Carrasco and Don Juan de Echarte.[16]

Cuevas, in his analysis of Iturbide's regime, felt that the government had been too lenient in dealing with these traitors and that his leniency in allowing the prisoners to have such visitors as Don Miguel Santa María and Joel R. Poinsett, who evidently had secret instructions which led to the conspiracy in the hope of gaining more territory for the United States through the intercession of the imprisoned deputies, who when freed, would be of aid to the United States.[17]

After Victoria's escape, he again found refuge at the hacienda of Francisco Arrillaga, Paso de Ovejas, near Veracruz. Arrillaga was a Spanish merchant who had always been sympathetic to the insurgents and who had evidently corresponded with them regularly. The insurgent general waited patiently for signs of amnesty from the government, but these were not forthcoming because Iturbide was bitterly opposed to Victoria's return to the capitol as an official representative, although no overtures were made to capture him and to return him to his jail cell.

Discussion continued on the type of government which should be set up to rule the nation. There was much interest in the constitutional provision as laid out in the French and United States constitutions (and after which some ideas in the Spanish constitution were patterned); some citizens wanted to support a monarchy headed by a Criollo such as Iturbide; while a third group sought strict execution of the _Plan of Iguala_ which stipulated the right to rule be restricted to the Bourbons of Spain.

While these political maneuvers were underway in Mexico, the Spanish Cortes nullified the Treaty of Córdoba on February 12, 1822. It really was not surprising that this treaty was turned down as it was in Spain's best interest not to give up this rich territory. When the Mexicans learned of this, it automatically evaporated the support of the Bourbonist faction but added to the strength of the Iturbidists. Since provision had been made in the _Plan of Iguala_ in the event that Ferdinand VII or a member of his family rejected the throne, this left the selection of a monarch in the hands of the legislature. It may be that Iturbide had anticipated this possibility and was prepared for the announcement, for he had set about extending favors and trying to ally many of the deputies of the government on his side. His ambition had no end in view except complete domination of the government by himself. He still desired to reign supreme.

According to Hall, "On May 18, 1822 Iturbide presented to the Congress two _Madrid Gazettes_ [sic] of the

13th and 14th of February, 1822 by which it appeared the Cortes of Spain had declared the Treaty of Córdoba to be null and void and totally disavowed his [O'Donoju's] acts."[18] He suggested to the Congress that it had to take some action on the selection of a ruler or again fall under the domination of Spain. The deputies were intimidated by Iturbide, but they took no immediate action.

However, the deliberations were soon to be taken out of their hands. On the night of May 18, 1822 a sergeant named Pío Marcha gathered together other sergeants, corporals and soldiers. He distributed some money among them and told them to go into the streets of Mexico shouting "Viva Agustín Primero." In a short time others in the streets took up the cry and as a result Iturbidists approached Iturbide and presumably put pressure on him to accept the throne. He modestly declined, but it did not require much persuasion to have him accede to being Emperor and to take on the leadership of the government of Mexico. It has been alleged that his money was the key that Pío Marcha used to open the door of Iturbide's bid for the monarchy; but no documentation was ever brought forward to prove the claim, though conjecture on the part of many persons conceded the possibility.

The fledgling Congress was reluctant to accept Iturbide and approve him as emperor, but there was a great clamor by the people and several times the doors of the chambers were stormed by protestors and the constituent body felt sufficiently threatened so that they finally decided they had the legislative authority to take action and called for a vote. In view of the unruly mob outside the chamber, the Congress gave seventy votes for the resolution to make Iturbide the emperor. There were fifteen votes against the resolution. The intimidated deputies had no choice except to proclaim Iturbide as the Emperor, Agustín I. This action was taken on May 22, 1822. He was invested in office in the midst of pomp and splendor in the Cathedral of Mexico on Sunday, June 22, 1822.[19]

The new emperor conferred on his wife and relations titles of nobility. He made his eldest son a prince with the right of succession. He organized the "Order of Guadalupe," an exclusive honorary to which only persons of high standing in Iturbide's list of supporters were admitted as members.

Agustín I continued his autocratic dictates after his attainment of the high office. His ambitious quest for power, coupled with the restraints of a recalcitrant and reluctant congress, created a continuous struggle for control. The hesitancy and lack of support of the legislative body of his programs made him impatient. His continuous meddling in the prerogatives of the group in the areas of constitutional provision and judicial control of the courts angered the deputies. When he requested the establishment of a military tribunal with dictatorial powers, the Congress rejected his mandate. He retaliated by arresting a number of the deputies on August 26 and 27, 1822, in an attempt to make them comply with his will. Not succeeding in these tactics, he sent General Luis Cortázar to disband the Congress on October 31, 1822. He then selected the Junta Nacional Instituyente of forty-five persons from among the more easily cowed members of the recent Congress.

From his refuge in the mountains, Victoria condemned the emperor as early as August 1, 1822. According to Callcott, who tells of Victoria's attitude, "stern old Guadalupe Victoria, his principles and characteristics reminding one of the gnarled heroes of the day glorified by Plutarch, issued a ringing proclamation to the people. He denounced Iturbide as a self-seeking tyrant, who had betrayed his principles for the sake of power."[20]

Bullock in his memoirs indicated Victoria was always against Iturbide and wrote about the insurgent general in this fashion: "A real well-wisher to the cause of rational liberty, coolness and determination in the hour of danger and an ardent desire to form a connexion with this country, have ever been the leading features of his character. The moment he considered the view of the ex-Emperor injurious to the rights of the people, he publicly denounced him. . . ."[21]

Meanwhile, the dismissed congressmen returned to their respective districts and added their voices to the dissension. They began haranguing about the despotism of Iturbide. Bravo and Guerrero were among those who returned to their provinces bitter about the attitude of the Emperor. Others around him began to become disenchanted with Iturbide and he began to lose the support of many of his closest followers.

Jealousies and intrigues within the army were the order of the day. The growing influences of the Masonic order, as well as disgust at the lack of personal rewards forthcoming from Iturbide--either by recognition as members of the Order of Guadalupe or receipt of public office, which many had expected for supporting him--lost him additional followers. The dissolution of the Congress hastened the decision of many of the malcontents to abandon Iturbide. This was especially true when they realized his intent was to be a dictator with sole power over the nation's activities. Oddly enough there was no immediate overt action taken to depose him.

Intrigues were rampant. The dissidents in the army allied with the malcontents of the dismissed Congress.

The Masonic lodges held meetings to discuss alternatives to attain control of the government; but there was a lack of a catalytic force. Little definite action was taken, speeches were rife, and the country was in a stage of stagnancy although it was apparent that many were again ready for rebellion. Perhaps everyone was tired of bloodshed and lacked hope to set up a workable representative government. There were really few persons who were experienced in self-government and who were cognizant of the statesmanship required to rule a nation emerging from the iconoclastic dominion of Spain.

Action finally came from an unexpected source. The disaffection arose from Coronel Antonio López de Santa Anna, who had been by-passed by Iturbide for the governor-generalship of the province of Veracruz. The honor had gone to General José Antonio Echávarri, whom Santa Anna detested. Santa Anna, a native of Jalapa, had coveted this post for himself. However, he had not succeeded in bringing in Victoria as directed by Iturbide, who wished to incarcerate him as he was still creating antagonism toward the government in the province of Veracruz. Santa Anna, according to Muñoz, secretly admired Victoria and made no real effort to arrest him. Santa Anna and Iturbide also had some difference in several business deals, in which some of Santa Anna's financial gains were detrimental to the Emperor's own interests. Iturbide disliked Santa Anna, who was courting Iturbide's elder sister, and often made him the butt of jokes. What rankled Iturbide most, however, was that Santa Anna had indulged in a plot against Echávarri, his commanding officer. The plot had backfired, and it was evident to Santa Anna that he was about to be chastised or even arrested for his erroneous ways.

Santa Anna's last plot was especially flagrant and seditious. Santa Anna had made overtures to General Francisco Lemaur at the Castillo de San Juan de Ulúa which would lead to the elimination of his senior officer, Echávarri. As a consequence he called on Echávarri and suggested a method of operation to breach the fort's defenses. Brigadier Echávarri was interested in the plan and agreed to participate. After the attack was launched, the Brigadier was nearly snared in the trap that had been set for him; but he escaped the encirclement and was able to retreat to safety. He realized at once Santa Anna's complicity and was bitter about his treacherous subterfuge. He sent without delay a dispatch to the Emperor. Iturbide was furious and left Mexico City to go to Jalapa to face Santa Anna. He planned to strip him of his post and to have him arrested.

Upon Iturbide's arrival, Santa Anna was summoned to

his presence, whereupon Iturbide subtly asked him to report to him for further orders in Mexico City. Hanighen says: "Santa Anna later asserted that he had been warned of his removal and that he feigned gratitude, asking only that he be given time to set his affairs in order. While he was seated at a table with the Emperor exchanging subtle prevarications, an aide-de-camp entered and sternly reminded Santa Anna that he was infringing one of the most sacred rules of the new Imperial code: 'In the Emperor's presence one should stand at attention.'"[22]

All these signs Santa Anna accepted as warnings that he was in disfavor with the Emperor and that his machinations had been uncovered. He took quiet leave and realizing that he was about to be stripped of his authority and that he was in disgrace and might momentarily be held for execution, he fled the city. His destination was Veracruz. There, surrounded by his troops, he declared for a republic against the tyranny of Iturbide. It is doubtful if he really knew much about a republican government, but he was urged on by Carlos María de Bustamante; and with the collaboration of this former congressional deputy and the aid of Miguel Santa María of the Columbian republic, he presented a document, the Plan of Veracruz. This article of freedom, consisting of seventeen statements detailing his plans for a new Mexican republic, he presented to the people of Veracruz.

Upon hearing of Santa Anna's proclamation, Victoria joined Santa Anna and working with him modified some of the statements and issued them jointly to the people of Mexico. Santa Anna's denunciation of Agustín I as a tyrant who was betraying the freedom of the people was emotionally charged and was well accepted by the Veracruzanos. The request for a return to order and reestablishing a republic was acceptable to many of those who were disillusioned with Iturbide's reign. It was not difficult to gain support for rebellion, especially with the backing of their hero, Guadalupe Victoria.[23]

Santa Anna, though not overly popular himself, was acceptable to the Veracruzanos on a limited basis; but it was most unlikely that they would have continued to support him had he not been joined by Victoria. It was repeatedly said of Santa Anna "that he used his friends as tools to achieve the power he continually sought for himself."[24] Santa Anna welcomed the guerrilla chief without reservation and realized that it was unlikely he would have support without the backing of Victoria, and even accepted the position as second-in-command after Victoria appeared on the scene. There were many persons that did not accept the ex-royalist officer at face value. They knew he had been one of the most violent of the royalists against the independence leaders and they insisted that Victoria be made the commander-in-chief of the new republican army. Though Victoria at first demurred, he accepted the position, realizing that he had the full confidence of the troops and the citizenry. Under his control the insurrection began to stabilize and more of the Mexicans outside of Veracruz began to rally to his support.

The army--taking the name of El Ejército Libertador --split into several units and marched out from Veracruz to win over more of the populace and to have them support the ideology of a republican government. The way to success was not to be easy and it ran into many obstacles before the liberating army would combine with other rebellious groups and eventually secure independence and a republican government for Mexico.

After his proclamation in Veracruz and the union with Victoria, Santa Anna's group departed with determination for Jalapa. His troops had some victories along the way, but after coming into contact with the combined forces of José María Calderón and Echávarri, his former superior and commandante of Jalapa, in the outskirts of that city, the liberating army led by Santa Anna was scattered and forced into retreat. Calderón would have shot the prisoners he captured as traitors; but Echávarri wisely discouraged this as he was afraid it might create some backlash toward the Emperor.

Santa Anna, having avoided capture, retreated rapidly toward Veracruz. Near the Puente del Rey (now Puente Nacional), he encountered Guadalupe Victoria with a force of about 300 men accompanying him. "All has failed, General," said Santa Anna, "We have taken the last gamble and lost. Let us go to the port where I have a brigantine waiting as part of the campaign, and we shall take off to a foreign port. We continue to be in grave danger here."

"Friend," responded Guadalupe Victoria, "You go to Veracruz to get in readiness and only when they present you with my head, will it be necessary for you to leave. But in the meanwhile, as I live, it would be to your honor to stay and to help defend the cause of liberty. And within one month, you can judge," he said, stretching out his hand with firmness, "all will change favorably for us."[25]

In spite of Victoria's confidence, the revolt was not to succeed immediately. Bravo and Guerrero, who had left Mexico City to fight in the south with the new army of liberation were both defeated in attempts to overcome Iturbide's troops. Guerrero was wounded and Bravo managed to escape to the mountains and went into hiding. Victoria was besieged in his favorite haunt at Puente del Rey, and Santa Anna, in a safe refuge in Veracruz, awaited the outcome of the fray.

Meanwhile other factors occurred which would result in the overthrow of Iturbide's regime. After Santa Anna's revolt, the Emperor had declared him a traitor and stripped him of his army rank and he promised pardon to the followers of Santa Anna if they would desert him. His pleas appeared to have little avail, especially since he was unable to apprehend Santa Anna. The Emperor appeared to be vacillating and began to realize that he was losing his hold on the rest of the army. Just as Apodaca had been betrayed by Iturbide, so was he abandoned by those to whom he had given his trust. Echávarri, influenced by Michelena and Ramos Arizpe, withdrew his support from Agustín I and, drawing other prominent officers about him, proposed a new plan for Mexico's freedom. Many of these new conspirators were members of the Escoseses Masonic lodges that had been gaining strength in Mexican politics and who were sympathetic to strengthening the power of the army and the church. These men would all play important parts in the further development of Mexican politics.

On the first of February, 1823 the new revolutionary group devised the Plan of Casa Mata, the name being taken from the city in which the meeting was held by leading army officials including Echávarri, Pedro Celestino Negrete, José Morán y Del Villar (Marqués de Vivanco) of Puebla, Coronel José María Lobato, Luis Cortázar Rábago and other imperialists who deserted Agustín I. The new leaders stated that their plan was to reinstate many of the old provisions of the Plan of Iguala, reestablish the Congress and to set up an Executive Power Committee. This junta of militarists had as its president Echávarri, with Miguel Calderón as his assistant, and an executive council. This group held meetings in Jalapa and invited Victoria and Santa Anna as well as the other chiefs, Bravo and Guerrero, to join them. All the rebels readily accepted the invitation with the exception of Guadalupe Victoria, who resolved not to cooperate until Iturbide was completely devoid of power. The junta had extended an invitation to Iturbide to abdicate his position and join the new movement; but the Emperor had tried to reassemble his hand-picked Congress and win their support. This subterfuge did not work and, realizing he could not muster any army support and hold his position, he abdicated on March 19, 1823.[26]

Former members of the elected congressional delegations were recalled to the capital and reinforced by the army they reconvened on March 29, 1823. There was a membership of one hundred deputies present and the body was declared a national assembly and provided for a provisional government retaining a military triumvirate of Nicolás Bravo, Pedro Celestino Negrete and Guadalupe Victoria. As Bravo and Victoria were often called upon to go to various parts of Mexico to quell disturbances and reaffirm the establishment of the government, two persons were chosen as alternates to act in their positions: Mariano Michelena and Miguel Domínguez.

Agustín I had hoped that after his abdication he would be retained in some respectable position of power, but he had few supporters left to him since most of them had deserted his cause for the new government. All proposals made by him to reassert his authority were to no avail. With his abdication went all his power and his friends. Even though his cause was lost, he bargained advantageously and won from his victors a liberal pension of $25,000 per year and other grants. However, fear of intrigue on the part of Iturbide led to a resolution by the Congress to exile him.

The former emperor protested bitterly at leaving Mexico and offered to stay in one of the more remote intendencies; but his request was not granted and he and his family with retainers amounting to approximately twenty-five persons were sent to Veracruz. As there were some of his enemies that felt that he was a menace to Mexican independence, he was heavily guarded first by Nicolás Bravo and then by Guadalupe Victoria.[27]

Victoria was very unhappy with his charge as the trip to Veracruz was beset with petty arguments, illness among his retinue, slow tedious movement because of the large amount of goods which the Iturbide party had brought, bad weather and other petty annoyances. However, no attacks were made upon the caravan and the party eventually reached the port of Veracruz.

Zavala writes that in spite of Victoria's aversion to the former Emperor, when Victoria took over the responsibility for Iturbide's journey to the coast that the two men met amiably. He describes the meeting as one of respect between two soldiers: "Señor Victoria, who was in charge of the ex-emperor's embarcation, treated him with the most conspicuous consideration. It is said that Iturbide after having shown his gratitude and demonstrated sentiments of appreciation of his character and constancy, gave him a watch, saying that he should receive it as a pledge of his regard. In reality, although Victoria was his enemy, he failed neither the promises nor oaths he had made previously, nor the respect due to the unfortunate, nor the consideration to which this unhappy Mexican had a right, for his service."[28]

Rivera Cambas, Mexican historian, in his description of the embarcation of Iturbide further states "that the ex-emperor after giving a watch to Victoria, accepted in return a shawl which the General gave him and placed it around his neck with a gesture of fondness."[29]

Iturbide and his followers left on May 11, 1823 on the ship, Rawlins, which took him directly to Leghorn, Italy after a leisurely sixty-day voyage. It was in this city that the Mexican government decreed that he should live on the pension of $25,000 which it had provided for him. However, the deposed monarch was restless in his exile and felt that his aid was needed in Mexico. He was determined to return to his native land and with this in mind, after several months he journeyed to England and from there, with a number of followers, he set forth to the Mexican coast. He did not realize that on April 28, 1824 the Mexican Congress had passed a decree making him an outlaw and an enemy of the state and that his presence in Mexico would lead to his death.

When he disembarked at Soto la Marina, he was accompanied by his aide-de-camp, a Pole by the name of Count Carlos de Beneski, and was unaware of his danger. Shortly after coming ashore, he was apprehended by General Felipe de la Garza, the commandante of Tamaulipas. The ex-emperor was taken to Padilla where the state congress was in session. Without any preliminaries he was sentenced to death and executed by a firing squad on July 18, 1824. He was buried at Padilla. In 1838 his remains were removed to the Cathedral of Mexico City, and later he was interred with other heroes of the independence in the Column of Independence on the Paseo de la Reforma in Mexico City.

As has been mentioned earlier, the triumvirate Executive Power Committee, which consisted of Bravo, Negrete and Victoria had been supplemented with Domínguez and Michelena, who assumed the duties of Bravo and Victoria since these two were out of the capitol most of the time. They had the tiresome duty of quelling revolts against the government and carrying out assignments asserting the authority of the new government in outlying provinces. Michelena became acting president of the country and when Domínguez became ill, chose Vicente Guerrero as a substitute on the roster of rulers.

It is interesting to note that the supreme power was in the hands of former insurgents such as Bravo, Victoria and Guerrero, but that the new congress which had been organized was in the hands of liberals such as Lorenzo de Zavala, Juan de Dios Cañedo, Valentin Gómez Farias and Miguel Ramos Arizpe, all young men who had not been deeply involved in the early fight for independence.

Shortly after the organization of the Executive Power Committee, Victoria left for Jalapa where he was authorized to meet with the Spanish Commissioners sent by the government of Spain to negotiate peace and commercial treaties with the Iturbidist regime. They had stayed in the Castillo de San Juan de Ulúa while the Iturbidists were in conflict with the revolutionaries led by Santa Anna and Victoria.

Bravo had been authorized to sit in with the Spanish Commissioners, along with Victoria, but he was busy with the insurrectionists in the South and the negotiations were left entirely in the hands of Victoria.

The Spanish Commissioners were Juan Ramón Oses, Santiago Irissari and Blas Oses, the son of Juan Ramón. He was secretary for the Commission. The three men were disenchanted with the dreary confines of the Castillo and were pleased to leave for Jalapa when the new government invited them to negotiate treaties on April 23, 1823.

On April 30, 1823, the Mexican Minister of Foreign and Interior Relations, Lucas Alamán, communicated with the Commissioners, sending his compliments to those persons whom he had known in Spain. In this letter he obliquely alluded to the negotiator, Guadalupe Victoria, as being incompetent and hoped that in spite of this dilatory character that negotiations would go well: a rather odd type of letter to be received from a Minister of a nation which was conferring with a group representing an old enemy and of a Minister who was about to embark upon an attempt to win friends in a rather hostile world.

This was not too surprising an attack on Victoria, since Alamán had taken an instant dislike to Victoria when he met him. It is quite obvious throughout Alamán's writings that he had nothing but contempt for Victoria. This dislike was continued in all governmental contacts and activities and it is strange that Victoria did not dismiss him. Alamán felt that Victoria was uncouth, dilatory, weak and uncultured, yet the insurgent leader had been for many years a law student and a tutor to many of the youth from the best families in Criollo Mexico. Yet, most allusions to Victoria in Alamán's history are in a rather deprecating tone. Perhaps Victoria's desire to tax heavily all large estates had something to do with Alamán's hatred as he was the caretaker of the huge Cortés holdings.

Correspondence transmitted to Victoria from the Congress on May 13, 1823, contained the following: (1) Agreement to listen to the terms of the Commissioners; (2) Official appointment of Victoria and Bravo as Commissioners for Mexico and (3) Approval of the examination of the credentials and willingness of the Congress to accept these credentials and to listen to propositions about peace and commercial treaties agreements.

Upon the receipt of the safe conduct authority by the Congress to travel from Veracruz to Jalapa, the

Commissioners with a small party journeyed through the jungle tropics for Jalapa where the negotiations were to be discussed. Victoria chose as his secretary for the conference the deputy from Veracruz, Don José María Serrano.

The conference has held in the Governor's Palace where there was first an extremely formal exchange of documents of recognition. Negotiations were begun on a rather cordial plane, but the harmony was not to last long. Complications arose, especially caused by Guadalupe Victoria, who insisted on the term of "absolute independence" being placed in the recognition agreement. Since Spain did not recognize Mexican independence, the leader of the Spanish Commissioners, Juan Ramón Oses, felt that his group did not have the authority to approve this phraseology. He suggested the word "provisional" be inserted. Victoria was adamant in his demands and finally the term "absolute independence" was inserted much to the dismay of Oses who pointed out that the Cortes was not likely to accept this point. June 13, 1823 was the memorable day when Victoria was able to sway Oses to give semi-recognition to the Mexican government and admit it was a sovereign nation. With this problem out of the way, negotiations were undertaken on the subject of commercial treaties.[30]

However, what appeared to be a victory for Mexico was not to be carried out in fruition. The Spanish and Mexicans had been for months squabbling about the sovereignty of the islet of Sacrificios. The Mexicans claimed this as their territory and had several soldiers occupying it. However, the Commandante-general of the Castillo de San Juan de Ulúa decided to occupy the islet in the name of Spain and sent a complement of troops over to overcome the Mexicans there. Victoria took a rather violent exception to this breach of truce by Francisco Lemaur and chided the Spanish Commissioners vociferously. In the correspondence which then took place between the Commandante-general and the Commissioners, the leader, Oses, was reassured by Lemaur that the Spanish held a legal right of possession to the islet and that he would not give up Sacrificios. The Spanish Commissioners accepted the decision and Victoria was furious. The result was a complete breach in the negotiations, especially after troops from the Castillo fired upon Veracruz while Mexican troops were being gathered in that port in an attempt to regain Sacrificios. This act resulted in a state of war and the lives of the Spanish Commissioners were endangered. However, on September 26, 1823 Victoria granted safe-conduct passports for the Spanish Commissioners, gave them an escort and had them leave for Alvarado from where they embarked for Cuba.[31]

On October 1, 1823, a copy of an official communication was sent to the Spanish government rupturing the relations between the Mexican and Spanish governments. It was signed by the Minister, Lucas Alamán, and declared the following: "Due to hostilities by the governor of the Castillo de San Juan de Ulúa against Veracruz, the Executive Power Committee consideres this an act of aggression to the nation and (1) They declare cutting all relations--political and commerical--with the Spanish nation; (2) the principles of the Mexican nation must call for an immediate embargo against Spanish commerce; (3) Any intercourse under way in Europe at this time will be terminated in four months; forty days for Havana; (4) Those agreements completed before the hostilities are not terminated until fulfilled as above; and (5) Imports will be admitted as agreed for four months from this date.[32]

Although the amicable relations between the two nations were ruptured, it was quite apparent that there were sufficient loopholes in the declaration to allow for limited imports so that Mexico would not be entirely isolated while it negotiated with other nations, especially with England and the United States. England, of course, had been generous in dealing with the Mexicans and had wooed them with special envoys throughout the revolution to keep their influence strong with Mexico.

After the collapse of the Spanish negotiations and prior to Victoria's return to Mexico City to fulfill his obligations on the Executive Power Committee, Victoria received Dr. Patrick Mackie of England often in his private quarters. Bullock tells of his discussions with Mackie and how the Englishman felt he was exerting a strong influence on Victoria to influence the Mexican leader in trading with England. Bullock wrote in his diary: "He [Dr. Mackie] was now executing the object of a mission to which he was entrusted by the British government, having fortunately met here General Victoria, the chief of the Executive Government, with whom he usually spent the evenings, without the object of his voyage being even surmised in the city. I have reason to believe that the Doctor's exertions were attended with complete success, and that the commercial interests between England and Mexico will be mutually benefited by them; especially as he was received by General Victoria, in his official capacity, with the greatest of pleasure, and his opinion of the advantages to be derived from a connexion with this country duly appreciated."[33]

The United States was interested in the new Mexican government as well, and had in 1822 sent as an observer Joel R. Poinsett to obtain a firsthand view of the independent government. His presence was regarded with suspicion as he consorted with several of the deputies whom Iturbide had sent to prison. They were regarded with suspicion as they were vociferous liberals. Poinsett was also a constant companion of Miguel Santa María of Columbia whom Iturbide later ousted from Mexico. The conservative element of the Iturbidists still in power considered the American ambassador as an enemy of the government and that he was conspiring with Santa María to encourage a more liberal government. They kept a diligent eye on his stay and were relieved when he left. This short official stay, however, was to be extended on his next journey to Mexico in 1825 when he returned to Mexico as the American ambassador plenipotentiary and became the center of controversy in the Mexican government.[34]

The formidable task of reorganizing the emerging nation continued under the watchful eyes of a new group of young politicians mingled with some of the early patriots who had fought for Mexican independence. Leaders included among the Federalists Miguel Ramos Arizpe and Valentin Gómez Farías as well as Carlos María de Bustamante, Ignacio Rayón, and Fray Servando Teresa de Mier. Conservatives in the government were led by Lucas Alamán and the Minister of War, an old enemy of Victoria, Manuel Mier y Terán. As long as Victoria and Bravo were out quelling riots and objections to the new government, there appeared to be little friction while the leaders in Mexico City did as they pleased. However, the peace was shattered when Victoria demanded accountability of the government. The strong animosities held by Alamán and Mier y Terán against Victoria again came to the front when Victoria remained in the capitol. Bancroft notes that "Victoria's presence in the government caused a material change, which gradually influenced subsequent events. He caused Arrillaga to be dismissed, in spite of the objections of Bravo and Dominguez, and of the Ministers Alamán and Mier y Terán. He received the support of Domínguez to place José Ignacio Esteva in charge of the national treasury, and immediately the appointment caused a rift in government affairs as the new Minister was an able, energetic and industrious man; but his chief fault was that he interfered unduly with the other departments, especially the Ministry of War, and made himself generally unpopular."[35]

There was much bitterness between all factions in the struggle between the conservative Centralists and the more liberal Federalists and it was difficult to set up a suitable government. The Centralists felt that the limited experience of the persons in government would make their type of structure more suitable to a nation accustomed to a strict regime, whereas the Federalists believed in a new spirit of freedom and self-rule. The Constitution of 1824 was being shaped in such way that there was of necessity a compromise in acceptance of certain ideologies of both parties. Victoria tried to satisfy both factions by appointing leaders from both sides in his cabinet. This action may have been influenced by the North American ideology of George Washington who used much the same type of compromise in his selection of the first cabinet. This move, however, appeared to be unacceptable to either group. In the draft and eventual acceptance of the constitution there were many unresolved issues which were to be a continuous source of serious contention for many years.[36]

The final draft of the Constitution of 1824 was influenced by the Declaration of Independence and the Constitution of its northern neighbor, the United States, but it had some phraseology from the Spanish Constitution of 1812 promulgated by the Spanish Cortes. There were features, especially in the extraordinary powers given to the president, which were strictly Mexican in origin. Nor did the Mexican Constitution set up trials by jury as in the American document.

The new laws of Mexico lacked some of the strong points suggested by the Congress of Anáhuac document, such as distribution of property, freedom of all classes, and full emancipation from slavery--as well as division of wealth and industry. The protection of the Catholic religion and, to some extent, the power of the Church was retained so that the lower classes did not gain much freedom. In many ways, the despotism of the Spanish nobility and the power of the merchants, government officials and the army were transferred into the hands of the landlords and Criollos who took over the reins of the government. It is easy to see that Victoria's early experiences in the various colleges in which he tutored and studied had some influence upon his acceptance of this more rigid structure, although he had been rabid in the desire for freedom for all peoples.

Bremauntz, in his study, states that the Constitution had many strong points and that it was rightfully slanted toward educating a new generation of leaders as well as establishing some freedoms formerly unknown to the Mexican people. The document creating new colleges of the Navy, Artillery and Engineers set up opportunities for the Criollos to control their own destinies, especially in giving permission to study the subjects of political economy and philosophies of other nations in the existing schools; and in creating a monetary system it gave the nation new freedom to seek out loans to rehabilitate the nation. Other reforms included provisions for building of roads and canals for better communication, establishment of a postal system

7. A painting of Guadalupe Victoria from the Museo de Historia del Castillo de Chapultepec. It has the caption, "Guadalupe Victoria, Yndividuo de esta Colegio (San Ildefonso, de la Real y Pontificia Universidad de México) y primer Presidente de los Estado Unidos Mexicanos.--Año de 1825." Photo by the author.

and aid to industry to overcome the destruction of the mines, to establish the rights of a free press and much other legislation essential to building a new nation.[37]

CHAPTER FIVE

THE PRESIDENCY

In June 1824 the new Mexican republic held its first constitutional election and placed in office as president Don Guadalupe Victoria who had won a clear majority of all the votes cast. In the vice-presidency, the Congress was required to cast its ballot for one of two candidates: Bravo or Guerrero since there was a lack of majority in the votes cast for these candidates. It selected Bravo.[1]

The Congress, in its anxiety to set up a workable government, swore into office both of these men--Victoria and Bravo--on October 10, 1824--five months prior to the time allotted by the Constitution which had stipulated the date of inauguration as April 1, 1825. It set the salaries at 36,000 pesos a year for the presidency and 10,000 pesos per year for the vice-presidency.[2]

In his inaugural address Victoria promised a just rule under the aegis of the divine providence and with the cooperation of the people. He assured them of future prosperity of the nation as that was the goal which he held close to his heart. He believed religion should neither teach superstition nor sink into licentiousness and reaffirmed his strong faith in Mexican independence, for which he would shed his blood, and his support of liberty, for which he would lay down his life.[3]

The new president was extremely optimistic about the new republic and its future, for as he took the oath of office the treasury was reputed to be down to approximately $40 in its coffers. There was no trade in existence, poverty was the order of the day, and, in spite of assurances of freedom for all, the Church and the army still exerted strong controls over the political destiny of the new nation.

The Mexicans were fortunate in having Victoria for their president as he really was firmly convinced that the nation would rise to the challenge of freedom, and that all factions would unite in peace to forge a new sovereign power that would be readily recognized by other nations throughout the world. Hanighen states: "In the midst of the numerous scamps, adventurers and opportunists who crowded the public stage of Mexico of that day, he stands out as a truly noble figure. Absolutely honest, he never profited financially from his office; scrupulous, he adhered loyally to the Constitution he had sworn to protect; and he sought to govern with justice leavened by mercy--a rare trait in the fierce struggles of that time."[4]

Frost says of this era: "The parties of the nation were occupied in forming themselves. Pronunciamentos were very frequent, but they gave little alarm to the government, which proceeded steadily in a manner gratifying to the Republicans."[5]

The first two years of the constitutional government were fairly serene. In spite of some rivalries in the formation of new laws, arguments about court activities, and attempts to set up treaties of commerce with the support of the English and the United States, the nation did make progress. Free trade made headway, new ports were opened at Mazatlán and Guiamas (now Guaymas) and the army was reduced. The soldiers were given half-pay as reservists thereby saving the need of keeping an active army occupied and placing needed monies into circulation. There was good reasoning in this action as the army could not be drastically cut since there was still a definite threat from Spain which retained a large fleet of ships in the Gulf and sizeable garrisons on the island of Cuba.

A Mexican navy was established with the aid of a British loan, and an active fleet was assembled. Victoria established treaties with England--after the Congress had some pressure put on it from the English--to quell the anti-Spanish revolt of a Mexican commander, Gral. don José María Lobato, who was endangering English relationships. Victoria asked the nation to establish pensions for the widows of Iturrigaray, O'Donojú, and Iturbide.[6] This was done by the Congress and was a gracious move on part of the poverty-stricken nation but was an action typical of the regime of the time.

Victoria, in an attempt to obtain support from the Holy See and to avert any overt attacks from the Holy Alliance, wrote to Pope Leo XIII in order to establish some contact with the Vatican. His approach was successful and he received a conciliatory letter from Pope Leo as follows: "Our particular character and the dignity to which without merit We have been elevated require that We do not interpose Ourselves in that which in no manner pertains to the government of the Church, and We content Ourselves in giving due thanks for the consideration which We have merited from you and congratulate Ourselves for the peace and harmony which You assure Us the Mexican Nation enjoys by God's Favor."[7]

Victoria, seeking the friendship of the United

States, wrote to President Monroe about the new Mexican Constitution which had just been sanctioned and related to him the news of the offices to which he and Bravo had been elected. He included copies of the Mexican Constitution and spoke of the fraternal and harmonious bonds which the two republics would have, and stated he looked forward to a valuable alliance.[8]

Close relationships were not hurriedly established between Mexico and the United States as there was distrust on the part of the United States government of the new sovereignty of Mexico. As a consequence, the Mexicans looked to the relationships established with England for support--which was rapid in its outreach. The British did much to aid Mexico in its tottering development as a nation. Even though they had a selfish motive in capturing the Mexican trade, the British were instrumental in setting the new nation on the road to recovery and solvency. England loaned Mexico monies to build up its depleted treasury, aided in reestablishing the mines which had been neglected, flooded or destroyed during the civil strife. It gave Mexicans advice on how to set up port activities and facilities and tried to create responsibility in Mexican officials in understanding the ways of making the ports active and teaching them the means of levying and collecting various tax duties effectively.

These activities were not an easy task, for bribery was rampant in the major ports and drained off most of the needed resources. There was multiple taxation of goods by the various provinces, through which goods were transported, resulting in a serious inflation of prices and hampering the free flow of needed materials.

The early days of the Republic were a period in which peace and unity were so desperately needed to bind all Mexicans together in the common cause of governmental cohesion. Yet this was not to be the case. Political leaders divided into two major groups influenced by the conflicting interest of Federalism versus Centralism, the questions of heavy taxation of estates and capitalists, expulsion of the Spanish and other similar selfish enterprises.

In his address to the Constitutional Congress on December 24, 1824 the President called for fraternity and harmony, responsibility for good laws and justice and protection of the innocent. He stressed the sacred trust of the liberty which the congressmen held in upholding the constitutional rights of the people and in leading the way to obtain the applause of all nations which would admire them for their exemplary, stable government.[9]

In spite of many pleas for unity by the President, there was little cooperation among the Congressmen. It was not long before the political scene was dominated by the secret Masonic societies at whose meetings governmental affairs were discussed and decided without airing the information publicly in Congressional sessions. The nation was being torn apart by decisions made unilaterally by these small groups.

The followers of the Yorkinos (York Rite Masons) were opposed by the Escoceses (Scottish Rite Masons). The latter group was led by the Vice-president, Nicolás Bravo. His chief supporters were Generals Negrete, Barragán, Echávarri and Filisola, most of whom had been Iturbide supporters. Guerrero and Esteva, former Escoceses, joined the Yorkinos in 1825 along with Zavala when the new lodges were established. Lorenzo de Zavala was one of the principal movers of the organization of the Yorkinos and extensive correspondence to Poinsett was undertaken by him. It was definitely Poinsett who was able to get the charter to set up the lodges from Thomas Kittera of Philadelphia. The letter from Kittera to Poinsett which is deposited in the collection at the Historical Society of Pennsylvania in Philadelphia is quite clear on the topic. Without doubt the President, Guadalupe Victoria, was interested in the Yorkino lodges to offset the power of the Escoceses and may have discussed the establishment of them with the ambassador. At any rate all this political intrigue within the lodges was disastrous for the government, with one group favoring the limited monarchy and centralism and constantly fighting for power with the liberals who favored the republican form of government and federalism. Victoria, in an attempt to create a cohesive coalition government, chose men from both factions for his cabinet. In this way he hoped to balance the ideas of dissent and to try to lead his officials to a common meeting ground to build up a strong government. This device--used by George Washington in placing Hamilton and Jefferson in his cabinet--is not uncommon even today. It is often used by the governments of "emerging" nations in order to place excellent men from opposing parties into the government in order to benefit the nation.

Victoria listened to his advisors conscientiously and took their advice literally if he felt it was beneficial to the nation, but he lacked tact at times and alienated the politicians in office when he saw through their schemes in which they sought personal gain or power. This was especially true when many of the politicians became involved in the struggles between the Masonic lodges. The situation became especially volatile when the American ambassador, Joel R. Poinsett, became involved.

Callcott, in his book on the connections between Church and state in Mexico during this period says:

> In the year 1826 Don José María Alpuche é Infante, curate of a parish in the state of Tabasco, and at the time senator for the same state, conceived the idea of organizing the York Rite in Mexico, an idea which was aided by Don Ignacio Esteva, the Minister of the Treasury; Don Miguel Ramos Arizpe, canon of the Cathedral of Puebla and first assistant (official mayor) of the Minister of Justice, Colonel José Antonio Méjia and other persons. The President of the Republic, General Guadalupe Victoria, entering into the project. Five symbolic lodges were at once formed and after they were established, Mr. Poinsett, Minister Plenipotentiary of the United States in Mexico, was asked if he might secure, through his friends, the regulatory letters of patents. Supporting this petition and receiving the commission to install the grand lodge, was the only intervention that this person had in the rite, for which he has been so much and so unjustly denounced.[11]

However, regardless of the connections of Mr. Poinsett and his influences in Mexican politics, the launching of the Yorkino lodges to combat the growing influence of the Escoceses appears to be one of the gravest errors of the administration of Guadalupe Victoria. The situation got out of hand and it was said that the President later regretted using his influence in starting the lodges, which he hoped would be used to build up the nation rather than to destroy it.

It has been intimated that Poinsett instigated interest in a York Rite lodge during the time he was in Mexico in 1822; however, no evidence has been substantiated to prove this. In discussing Poinsett's influence Arrongoiz states: "Poinsett secured aid through the imbecile Victoria, who adopted his project. Zavala, Alpuche, and Ramos Arizpe participating . . . . Poinsett had arrived in Mexico at the time of Iturbide, who, informed whom the Anglo-American was, made him leave the country."[12] At this time no mention was made of setting up lodges of the York Rite. However, there had been some masons active in the early colonial period established under the Scottish Rite and prominent laity and clergy had been active in the lodges. First steps in the lodges' affiliation with political activites were apparently begun about 1813 in Mexico City.

Richard Greenleaf states that first evidence of masonry was revealed in 1760 when Juan María Reynaud gave testimony in Mexico City to the effect that there was an active Masonic group. Other trials were held by the Inquisition in the years to follow, but no major prosecutions seem to have been conducted. Greenleaf says: "It appears that the religious and political posture of Masonry in Mexico during the revolutionary era, 1808-1820, was conditioned by the Spanish political climate rather than the independence movement per se. Trials for the years 1811-1820 always picture Masonry as a subversive and insurrectionary force. Probably the lack of trials before 1811 suggests that Masonry was pro-royalist, and the Inquisition did little to suppress the movement, especially since many of its members were army officers.[13]

Presuming that the pro-loyalists were active in Masonry, it is not surprising that few of the early insurgents were involved in the movement as their aim was independence, which was anathema to the loyalists. There is no evidence that leaders such as Guadalupe Victoria were connected with any type of lodge activity prior to the 1820s. It was only after Nicolás Bravo became affiliated with such royalist army officers as Echávarri, Negrete and Filisola that he became involved with the *Escoceses*. The major national growth of this group did not occur until 1824 and the establishment of the *Yorkinos* came after Victoria was president in the latter part of 1825.

Bremauntz feels that the establishment of the *Yorkino* lodges was beneficial to Mexico as they "pressed anti-clerical legislation and liberal and progressive ideas against the power of the Church, founded important periodicals and took an active interest in all functions of the government in trying to improve the social and political welfare for the benefit of the Mexican nation. The struggle between the two opposing lodges ended with Bravo's defeat and the *Yorkinos* triumphed assuming the formation and progression of a liberal party."[14]

Several Mexican historians were not of the same opinion and derided strongly the lodges and Poinsett whom they accuse of meddling in Mexican affairs. They claim that the *Yorkinos* were openly supported by Joel R. Poinsett, Minister Plenipotentiary from the United States who arrived on June 1, 1825 and promptly threw himself into Mexican politics.

Mariano Cuevas claims that the first York Rite lodge was established in Mexico City by Poinsett, who obtained a charter for the organization of the unit from Thomas Kittera in Philadelphia after it had been refused by a New York chapter. He cites evidence obtained from a photocopy of the original conserved in a letter in the records of the Pennsylvania Historical Society.[15]

Cuevas goes on to state that "on September 29, 1825 that Poinsett installed the leaders of the 'Gran Oriente Yorkino' in his home with the assistance of the

President (Victoria), the Minister of Hacienda (Esteva) and the Minister of Justice (Arizpe) and other dignitaries of that secret society. . . ."[16]

Fuentas Mares goes even farther and accuses Guadalupe Victoria of conspiring with Poinsett to set up the lodges in Mexico to combat the growing power of the Escoceses. He reiterates that if Victoria had any trepidations about Poinsett's activities, it was because he feared the revelation by Poinsett of the conspiracy in which he and Lorenzo de Zavala were involved in attempting to control Mexican political power.[17]

There is no reason to deny that Victoria would undertake any action that would be beneficial to his beloved Mexico and support of the York Rite lodges to further the political aims of his party would not be unreasonable. However, he withdrew his support of the lodges upon observing the extent of the desperate actions undertaken by the participants in order to obtain power and to prostitute the republican government to their own selfish interests which were undermining the effectiveness of the government. He had never been partial to secret societies, particularly abhorring the Scottish Rite lodges, and later lamented his own weakness in patronizing the York Rite lodges, as the country had been belittled by their actions.[18]

The British Minister, Henry G. Ward, had been part of a commission sent by Canning to Mexico in the autumn of 1823. He had made contact with Guadalupe Victoria in Veracruz while the city was still under seige from the Castillo de San Juan de Ulúa. At that time he received an extremely cordial welcome from Victoria and was aided in procuring personnel for the trip to Mexico City and return to the port city. Consequently, upon his return to Mexico City in 1825, Ward had made some political headway with Victoria prior to the appearance of Joel R. Poinsett in Mexico City on June 1, 1825. Ward had evidently been careful not to become too embroiled in the battle between the lodges and retained much influence with Victoria and became extremely friendly with Lucas Alamán.

British relations had always been good and contacts with the officials of the government cordial. The British interests in the mining concessions led to discussions about restoration of the damaged and flooded mines. Some of this talk had occurred during meetings between Dr. Patrick Mackie and Victoria as early as 1823 when Mackie was in Jalapa. Victoria, anxious to have his government obtain financial considerations, had pushed the restoration of the mines as an official of the triumvirate.

As a result of these past talks, Ward sought to consolidate his position and pressed the Minister of Foreign Relations, Lucas Alamán, for more favorable action. Alamán because of his own personal interest in mining and restoration to profit of the Cortés estates which he managed, negotiated some contracts with Ward.

Poinsett, realizing Ward's influence on Victoria, began to court the interest of the Vice-president, Bravo. As time passed, this annoyed Alamán who felt that the American was by-passing him and that he was about to lose some advantages in the mining trade. Even more important was the influence which the shrewd American began to exert indirectly on the President and which was to have devastating results later.

For a time the gestures of friendship of Poinsett to the Mexican President were ignored by that leader; but Ward suggested it might be diplomatic to lend a sympathetic ear to the American ambassador. Why Ward made this suggestion is not apparent. He may have regretted his suggestion often at a later date as Poinsett's influence on the President and Mexican politics were to have regrettable effects. It was not known to Victoria that while the American Ambassador flattered him on the one hand, that Poinsett in his letters to Washington made it quite evident that he was rather contemptuous of Victoria.

As the plot unfolded, the contest between the two ambassadors for Victoria's attention led to some serious complications in Mexican politics as well as in the personal activities of the two rivals. Henry B. Parkes claims that Ward went to any extreme to exert his country's benevolence upon Mexico, even to the extent of paying particular attention to the alleged mistress of Victoria, the Countess de Regla.[19]

Even Poinsett conceded the influence of this official hostess of the President's Palace for he wrote to Henry Clay on October 12, 1825 the following: "The Countess of Regla . . . is a pretty Creole possessed of great shrewdness and exercising great influence over Victoria to turn out Don Pablo de la Llave, the Minister of Justice and Ecclesiastical Affairs and to appoint the Bishop of Puebla in his place."[20] Unfortunately there is little documentation on the Countess and the length of time and manner of her influence cannot be measured.

There was one person, however, whose influence on the Mexican President was very great. This was the staunch liberal, Fray Servando Teresa de Mier y Noriega Guerra. The ecclesiast lived in the National Palace and was the confidante of the President. It is to him that many of the reforms that Victoria carried out are attributed. Mier had sought strong reforms including distribution of property, creation of a strong democracy with complete sovereignty from Spain and avoidance of the entangling alliances which appeared apparent in the influences of Ward and Poinsett. Alamán fought the tenets of Mier with a strong passion and it was after Mier's death and the resultant struggle for the power of authority left void that created such problems for Victoria. Mier had never sought personal gain but was chiefly concerned for the benefits to Mexico that were sorely needed. Now with his demise those seeking to influence Victoria clamored for his attention and in his complete trusting manner was often led astray in making wise decisions since some of his advisors were more concerned about personal gain than in the good of the nation.

It was a most trying period for the President. He wanted to be friendly with the young nation to the north since that government had undergone some of the trials that his nation was currently undergoing, but so many of the Mexican leaders distrusted Poinsett and the way the Americans were expanding into Texas that he was in a constant dilemma of wondering whose advice he could trust.

Manuel Mier y Terán was actively opposing Victoria's policies and bringing to his attention the dangers of the immigration policies that were in effect. Many foreigners were moving into Texas. Some of this growth had been created by the Spanish government during the independence movement. The Spanish had liberalized the immigration laws and had opened the Texas territory and many new settlers had moved in. Immigration had also been approved by Iturbide's regime in the hope of keeping Spanish influence from the newly aligned borders. The United States acquisition of Florida in 1819 and subsequent purchase of Lousiana from the French was now creating a new type of problem. The new nation was in danger of losing part of its country.

After the Spanish had liberalized immigration into the Texas territory, the Spanish Ambassador, Luis de Onís, had been disturbed by the influence of the Americans in Texas and by the aid that the insurgents were getting from the American freebooters in New Orleans. Traders and freebooters were more than happy to ship supplies and ammunitions to the ports of Nautla and Boquilla de Piedras. There was a good profit involved in this and many persons willing to supply the revolutionists with all types of aid as long as the revolutionists could pay the price.

Even at times when payments were not promptly made, Mexican representatives such as Herrera did succeed in getting support for the Mexican cause in the 1814-1816 period, although the republican government--including Victoria's administration--would be plagued for years by American creditors seeking payment for goods delivered to the insurgents during the fight for Independence.[21]

During Victoria's reign, although he wanted to be friendly to the United States, there were many factors that were to lead to distrust of this northern neighbor. The burgeoning giant to the north was settling in disputed territory. One of the reasons for Poinsett's unpopularity with the Mexicans was his persistence in trying to settle the boundary between the United States and Mexico. In order to cope with this question, President Victoria had appointed Manuel Mier y Terán as head of a commission to aid in settling the border problem. The commission was delayed by internal strife and did not start its studies until 1827. Mier y Terán's recommendations eventually led to some agreements in 1828 and later legislation on April 6, 1830 to close the immigration processes allowed by the Spanish and Iturbide; but the damage to Mexican security of Texas lands was already beyond repair and conflicts led to interborder warfare.

The first concrete cause of Mexican anxiety had arisen from the action of immigrants who had rebelled against the Mexican domination toward the end of 1826. This revolt known as the Fredonian rebellion was the result of an attempt of incoming Americans to overthrow old land grants. On April 15, 1825, Haden Edwards obtained a contract under the state colonization laws to settle 800 families on his grant including Nacogdoches and the surrounding territory. Edwards moved into the territory and tried to evict the established inhabitants who, unfortunately, had not completed titles on their land. Many were threatened with dispossession and eviction unless they agreed to pay Edwards a sum of $520. in American currency. In consequence of complaints by the Mexicans and protracted correspondence with the political chiefs and the governor, Edwards, impatient with the delays, began to take over the land. President Victoria intervened with an order of annulment of Edwards's grant, and ordered his expulsion from Texas. Edwards resisted the action and with the aid of some Cherokee Indians defied the order and established the Fredonian republic which he set up on December 16, 1826.

It was a troublesome period for the new republic and its president. In the course of correspondence leading to the annulment of the Edwards contract, the political chief at San Antonio had dinned into the ears of the governor the suspicion that Edwards's ultimate purpose was to secede and carry his grant to the United States. The governor repeated the suspicions to Victoria and there, at the President's ear, was the British ambassador, Ward, pointing to the Fredonian rebellion as a complete confirmation of his prophetic warning that Poinsett and the United States were not to be trusted. Is it any wonder that Victoria was torn asunder in his attempts to set up a good government and yet keep good relationships between his supporters in Great Britain and the United States? Pressures were being placed upon him by Secretary of State Henry Clay and President John Quincy Adams to negotiate the boundary problem and his own ministers intimidated him to use force to keep boundaries intact. Finally he sent a garrison of soldiers to Nacogdoches in June 1827 to force peaceful co-existence. This was the first defensive action undertaken to protect the sovereignty of the Texas province which was about to be dominated by the settlers from the United States. Upon arrival at Nacogdoches the first duty of the commandante, Colonel Piedras, was to see that the immigrants bore passports, fulfilled character requirements, and that no one settled in unauthorized areas, a task that was not to prove fully successful.

The complications with the United States and England were not Victoria's only trouble spots. He had some political differences with the Holy Alliance when he encouraged the movement for the freedom of Cuba and lent his support to the freedom society, _Aguila Negra_, which was intriguing against Spain. When the plot was uncovered, Victoria was censured by the Holy Alliance. The United States also protested but intimated that if anyone was going to take over the island of Cuba, it would like to be the recipient.[22] Victoria's interest in freedom for Cuba was to decrease Spain's domination of the Caribbean, and its threat to the Gulf ports.

Naturally, no further action was taken by anyone and the plot was abandoned, but Victoria was accused by his political enemies of placing his country in jeopardy, even though he had some support from other members of the government for the idea of liberating the island from the grasp of the Spanish. After all, Spain was still an enemy of Mexico, and it had not yet recognized the independence of the republic. If a coup freeing Cuba from Spain could have been accomplished, this would have forced Spain out of the Caribbean and the Gulf of Mexico and put an ocean between the garrisons of Mexico and Spain. It would be a great advantage to the fledgling nation to have Spain's activities confined to the mainland.

Victoria had pressures put upon his regime from all directions. Any activity which he undertook was a politically hazardous project. Every piece of legislation had to be carefully weighed as to what the ultimate effect would be on the struggling nation. One example of his difficulties was an attempt on the part of the liberals to declare an extremely heavy tax on the landowners and the Church. Victoria refused to cooperate on this issue--being strongly influenced by Alamán, who as an administrator of the Cortés estates, felt that such action would be confiscatory--and, as a result, the president was severely criticized for protecting the wealthy.

Why Victoria listened to Alamán's advice has been questioned by Mexican historians for Alamán had never been a staunch supporter of the independence movement and had always been overly critical of Victoria. He considered the President a boor, uncouth, unpolished and bad-mannered. Yet Victoria tolerated Alamán and was influenced by him. Perhaps the thought of his country's welfare meant more to Victoria than anyone's personal opinion of him. He needed the services of a well-educated and able diplomat and he felt that Alamán filled the need.[23]

Critics were also plentiful when Victoria's government resorted to borrowing heavily from England in order to put the government in a favorable fiscal position. Ward was very much in favor of this action and worked closely with Alamán on the mining and commercial concessions. Ward influenced several commercial concerns in England to lend Mexico large sums of money in order to create solvency in Mexican coinage. Much of the money obtained from abroad was depleted by the high usury rates. However, one of the side benefits was the purchase of some ships and creation of the Mexican navy. The vessels used in conjunction with a strong land force from Veracruz was of sufficient strength to aid in capturing the Castillo de San Juan de Ulúa from the Spanish on November 18, 1825. These ships were used to transport the Spanish commander, José Coppinger and his Spanish troops to Cuba. The successful capture of the Fort, a troublesome burr in the harbor of Veracruz, was viewed as a great victory by the Mexican nation. Credit for the elimination of the last remnants of Spanish authority on Mexican soil must go to Miguel Barragán, the commandante of Veracruz and to Commodore David Porter of the Mexican navy.

The Mexican nation rejoiced at the defeat of the Spanish and extinction of the stronghold at Veracruz. It made them feel safer with the nearest Spanish garrison and fleet at Cuba instead of a few miles from the mainland of Mexico. Yet, the trials of the new nation were far from over. Problems of a different nature came up.

Victoria had been beseiged by many of the more conservative to change officers in his cabinet. The result was that there were constant turnovers in the government. Very little stability was gained in its operations. The press in Mexico City took sides and broadsides of all types were directed to the government. One of them published July 13, 1826 was influential in changing the government to a more liberal stand and placing into power Zavala, Esteva and the ecclesiastic, José María Alpuche é Infante. The result was that stronger demands were made by these leaders for the expulsion of the Spaniards from Mexico.

At a time when financial aid and unity of the nationals was needed they chose instead to fight among themselves and many of the deputies in the Congress continued to agitate against the Spanish and their expulsion. Victoria was not in favor of this since he recognized that these were the persons who still controlled most of the capital of the country. This factor was ignored and violence was committed against the Spanish daily and they began a quiet exodus. It was not helpful that some of the remaining Spaniards did plot against the government and when a conspiracy by Padre Joaquín Arenas against the nation was discovered the cries of the Criollos to oust the Spanish were louder than ever. The chief leader in the outcry for expulsion was the insurgent leader Vicente Guerrero. He demanded the arrest of Echávarri and Pedro Celestino Negrete who were involved in Arenas's plot to overthrow the republican government; however, Victoria had them exiled rather than executed. The plot had been revealed by General Ignacio Mora, commandante of the federal district who had been invited to participate. As a result of this latest move against the government, the Mexican legislature pushed a bill to expel the Spanish in December, 1827; but Victoria managed to squash the action. He was very severely criticized for his tolerance as most persons felt that Arenas's plot to overthrow the republican government and restore the monarchy was caused by the Spanish merchants. Victoria's sense of justice in some ways was to be his downfall in later years. It would have been easier for him to execute Arenas and his conspirators immediately and prevent further danger to his government. As Beaufoy points out:

> Amiable as his motives have been, I am inclined to think he has carried his clemency and adherence to legal forces further than was warranted either by sound discretion or sound humanity; for in all popular commotions or secret conspiracies, the prompt punishment of a guilty individual may spare the future shedding of much blood. In the case of Padre Arenas it would have been best to hang him.
>
> But I postively know, that when this proceeding was recommended to Victoria, he replied: "I am first president of the Republic, and I will not be the first to throw contempt on its laws, however deserving they may be of repeal; the prisoner shall be permitted to make use of all his privileges, and of every legal objection, but once condemned, I will order him to execution should it be my last hour of authority."[24]

It was at this time of crisis that another blow was received by the fledgling government. This was the collapse of the financial empire of Barclay and Company of England in 1827. There was a balance of $2,250,000 of the loan contracted with the company and the loss of the money was a tragedy to Mexican finances. Coupled with this was the loss of four million dollars which the Congress had borrowed in November 1827, having pledged revenues from customs and taxes on tobacco, which did not materialize. The nation suffered, not only from these extreme deficits, but had to suspend payments of debts and dividends to their other creditors in the world market and consequently the nation lost the confidence of various bankers and capital was not forthcoming from any sources under these conditions.

Pressures against the government were building up in the political activities of various members of the army. Santa Anna--a constant trouble-rouser in the capital--had been appointed as governor-general of Yucatán in the hope of lessening his influence in the government's internal affairs. The subterfuge worked for a time but Santa Anna did not like being so far from the center of activity and toward the end of 1825 had requested to come back to Mexico City. His request was granted with some reluctance, but it didn't turn out too badly as he spent several years on his plantation, Mango de Clavo, in the province of Veracruz.

However, the peaceful life was not for the general and he requested another army assignment which was granted. This was unfortunate as he soon became again a center of contention.

Santa Anna, along with Barragán and Ramos Arizpe, were creating real difficulties. Arizpe, who had made suggestions as early as 1824 to deprive the Spaniards of their governmental offices again began chewing this bone. As has been mentioned, Victoria was not sympathetic to this cause. He respected the rights of the Spaniards and their financial strengths and was very fair in his protection of them and demanded justice in carrying out means to protect them. This was evident as early as 1824, when he was able to quell the insurrection of the León brothers, Manuel and Antonio, after the Lobato revolt in Oaxaca in which the expulsion of the Spaniards was demanded. Victoria had taken some troops to the area after the ruthless murder of the Spanish tax collector of Huajuapán, Cayentano Machado. The revolt was stopped without additional bloodshed. "This happy result increased the esteem in which Victoria was held by all his countrymen," according to the historian, Alamán.[25]

Now, as in the past, Victoria was ready to stop the movement to expel the Spaniards. He was not hostile to them by the mere fact of nationality. He had, on the contrary,shown favor to many of them who served under him. He abhorred supporting severe measures against them, and only did so when his ministers presented the necessity of such measures for the safety of the nation, and indeed even of the Spaniards themselves, whose lives were often in great peril from popular violence. It was difficult for the government to guide the masses into the path of righteousness and justice which the President felt should be followed. He had been able to carry out justice in the murder of Machado as the guilty parties, Sergeant Trinidad Reina and Guadalupe La Madrid were executed, even though the two León brothers were exonerated.

In all cases where possible, the President tried to aid the Spaniards but often his officers ignored him as did the army leaders, Barragán and Santa Anna who gained support from Bravo and others and under the Montaño Plan in 1827 asked for four basic laws to be passed by the Congress. These were: (1) suppression of the secret societies; (2) dismissal of the Cabinet; (3) strict fulfillment of the Constitution; and (4) the dismissal of Poinsett.

Vice-president Bravo went to Tulancingo to coordinate the activities of those rebelling aginst Victoria, but he was soon overcome by the forces of Vicente Guerrero, whom Victoria sent out to subdue them. Bravo, Barragán and Gabriel Armijo were brought back to the capitol, but the Congress granted them amnesty, refusing to execute them as provided by law. Instead, the three were exiled from Mexico. The result of all these actions brought the expulsion of the Spanish to a certainty when Congress passed the law to this effect on December 20, 1827.

Guadalupe Victoria tried his best to gain the most advantageous benefits for his beloved Mexico. He stood alone in most of his activities as he tried to be a mediator between the powerful leaders in his government. His was a losing battle. As was indicated earlier, even his own vice-president rebelled against him.

Hanighen says of Bravo:

> Unhappily, with him [Victoria] was elected as vice-president his opponent for the Presidency [Bravo], a practice which led to disastrous results in later years and which almost upset his own reign. His electoral spouse, Nicolás Bravo, was an old patriot too and almost as popular as Victoria, but he believed in a centralized government with the states under the thumb of Mexico City, while Victoria believed in a loose federal system. Bravo was supported by the conservatives, clericals and Spaniards. They opposed Victoria's adherents who were mainly democrats, radicals, and critics of the Church.

> Perhaps the President's was an unwise program in view of Mexico's political experiences, but it was undoubtedly the popular choice not only of the mass of the people--that is those who could understand what it was all about--but especially of the rabid Jacobins, the anti-Spanish fanatics and of all the provincial _jefes_ who wanted to keep their power. Such was the division of forces, and the various adventurers chose the side which they thought would win and interposed their demoralizing on one side or the other.[27]

During all of these conflicts, officers in the Cabinet were constantly being changed. In the period from October 10, 1824 until the end of Victoria's term on March 19, 1829, there had been seven men as head of the Departmento de Relaciones Interiores y Exteriores; three as head of the Justicia; seven as chiefs of Guerra y Marina, and six as the leaders in the Departmento de Hacienda.[28] Is there any wonder that the government was able to operate at all? This constant turmoil in governmental affairs was not conducive to stability. Some of these men going from one agency to another extended their influences and disunities broadly. This was especially true of Gómez Pedraza and Esteva.

In the elections held in 1828, the so-called "correct, proper, and better people" supported Manuel Gómez Pedraza.[29] He was a Spanish officer during the fight for independence; and he was military commander at Huasteca before the empire. An ardent supporter of Iturbide, he had served during the Emperor's reign as the commandante-general of Mexico. With his pure Criollo background and popularity he was expected to be an easy winner. However, the _Yorkinos_ had split in their support and part of them supported instead Vicente Guerrero.

Victoria, Arizpe, and Esteva were the chief advocates for Pedraza, while Guerrero was favored by Alpuche, Zavala and propagandized by Joel R. Poinsett. When Pedraza was declared the winner of the election, Guerrero--backed by the ever-dissenting Santa Anna--accused the _Yorkinos_ of rigging the election and stirred rebellion in the capitol city. Victoria sent General Rincón against the dissident group, but he was powerless against the combined forces of Guerrero and Santa Anna. The President, in order to avoid a civil war, recalled General Rincón.

Congress was angry at the President and spoke of him in a derogatory fashion. Oddly enough a reply came not from Victoria, but from Guerrero who stated: "Many of the Congressional deputies were an infamous set of pickpockets and scoundrels; that if they did not take care, he would call his friends around him, and hang some twenty lawyers and priests; fellows who dared to call Victoria, himself, and others, by whom Spanish oppression had always been resisted--while they crouched to the lash--insurgents and mutineers."[30] In spite of his differences with Victoria, Guerrero respected the President for his intense love of his country and for the service he had rendered to it in the past. It was one of the many paradoxes of the time, for if Guerrero and Victoria could have cooperated more fully some of the tragic occurrences that were coming up could have been avoided. However, it had been similar circumstances of dissension that had made the war for independence last more than a decade and nearly defeated it entirely.

While Victoria was trying to avoid further bloodshed in subduing Guerrero and Santa Anna, a crushing blow to his government came from another quarter. Don Lorenzo de Zavala, governor of the State of Mexico, and an avowed enemy of Gómez Pedraza, directed his energies toward getting Guerrero in office, but he refused to unite with Santa Anna of whom he did not approve. Instead through trickery and bribery he contrived to get control of the La Acordada, the arsenal of Mexico City and audaciously checkmated the government of Guadalupe Victoria and indirectly aided Santa Anna, whose troops were able to overcome those of the government.

Bancroft described the events of the day: "then pillage was the order of the day. The leperos, taking advantage of the situation, raising the old cry--'¡Mueran los Españoles!'--rushed to the Parian, where the stores of the Spanish merchants were located, broke open the doors and ransacked it."[31]

Victoria went in person to the La Acordada to try to stop the rioting and pillaging in the capitol city, but his attempts were in vain. In the meanwhile, Gómez Pedraza, rather timid in his defense of the election and refusing to set off a bloody civil war, renounced his election as the President and fled the country on March 2, 1829.

Zavala went in to discuss the situation with President Victoria, who capitulated to the opposition, agreeing to install Guerrero as Minister of War in Pedraza's place. Later, under circumstances which could not be altered without grave consequences to the continued sovereignty of the government of Mexico, the Congress was compelled to overthrow the legal vote and to name Guerrero as the incoming President of the Republic within days of Gómez Pedraza's abdication of his responsibilities.

Zavala, when he discussed the current situation with the President, pointed out that the entire situation was very bleak. The liberal leader described the meeting: "at about ten in the morning, the activities of rebellion having ceased, I went in to see Victoria with several of my associates. A sepulchral silence reigned over the vast capitol of Mexico. In all the Palace there was no one but Victoria, who had been abandoned by his servants. Many warehouses had been ransacked, merchandise lay scattered on the streets and the plazas. There was not a sound to be heard in the streets except the clocks tolling the time. The whole atmosphere was one of fantasy. What a night; what a terrible night!"[32]

The coup-d'état of the liberals set a precedent for Mexican politics. Presidents were to be unseated every time someone was unhappy with a government edict, and the chief wasp in this hornet's nest of Mexican politicians was the unconquerable Santa Anna. He was without doubt the most prominent cancer in the sick political body of Mexico for the two decades which followed the foundation of the Mexican republic.

Don Guadalupe Victoria left office on the last day of March 1829, terminating his official duties extremely disheartened with the current disagreements in the government. He had been deserted by all and his dream of a successful, prosperous and peaceful government was in ashes.

Victoria was to be the only president of the Republic of Mexico to have held his elective office for the constitutionally prescribed time of four years without being deposed. After Guerrero assumed office, no president lasted very long. Between 1829 and 1863 thirty-two different men held the nation's highest office. Don Antonio López de Santa Anna held the position at intermittent periods eight times. The fate of the presidents through the years varied from exile to death, with the first fatality being Vicente Guerrero. He was shot for treason to the government when he rebelled against the Bustamante regime in 1831. Don Anastasio Bustamante had been vice-president during the short reign of Guerrero. Along with Guerrero the military executed Francisco Victoria, brother of the former president. He had been one of Guerrero's staunchest supporters, having preferred to stay with the veteran campaigner. He had little contact with his eminent brother during most of the years in which they fought for independence as their areas of operation had been very different.

CHAPTER SIX

VICTORIA: THE ENIGMA

Unlike our own first president of the United States, George Washington, the Mexicans do not pay lavish tribute to the first president of Mexico, Guadalupe Victoria. Strangely enough, there appears to be a negligent attitude toward this man and his life-long devotion to his country and to the many sacrifices he made to bring about independence. As a matter of fact, extensive documentation about Victoria is not easily culled in the vast history of Mexican independence. Lucas Alamán and Carlos María de Bustamante, the chief chroniclers of Mexican history during this period are more inclined to castigate the rebel chief, accusing him of every bad characteristic as a president; yet on occasion they reluctantly admit that he was an able leader, a true patriot, and one of the few persons who could have brought together the peoples of Mexico into a solidified unit of power.

At one time Bustamante had enough respect for Victoria to act as his counsel during the crisis with Iturbide. Even Poinsett, while working with Victoria, on the one hand, criticized him as an incompetent, on the other. Yet the American ambassador gained many concessions for the United States while Victoria was in office. These persons may have considered that Victoria was a feeble public figure, but he was respected by the masses for his courage, his forthrightness and his constant concern for the welfare of his country.

Victoria did take a leading role in shaping the Republic. His courage in speaking out against Iturbide, his efforts in behalf of the nation during his talks with the Spanish Commissioners and his extreme popularity in the elections of 1824 showed the support of the nation in his behalf. His directions to the states in pleading for amnesty for those who revolted against the government during the reign of the Supremo Poder Ejecutivo showed that he has aware of the problems involved in setting up a transitional government. He was aware that this time would be one of trial and experimentation of a democratic government which was ill-suited to the inexperienced Mexicans who were accustomed to a despotic and tyrannical government which had subjugated the natives for a period of three hundred years. Few of the persons who assumed the leadership of the nation had any instructions or experiences passed down to them as to how to operate a republic.

The history of the early years of Mexican independence places more emphasis on such divisive personalities as Santa Anna, Alamán, Ramos Arizpe, Iturbide, Zavala, Esteva and others than on the idealist, Victoria, who never betrayed the ideals of freedom and justice in which he believed. The same cannot be said of some of the leading figures in Mexico during that period. Many of them were more concerned with fulfilling their political and financial aims at the cost of the government and the unity of the nation.

Victoria's popularity with the masses did not fail until the late 1820s with the fall of the La Acordada and the rape of the Parian. During his residency, most of his dealing with the populace was considered fair and benign. One hundred years after he left office, he was eulogized in a pamphlet for contributing to the abolishment of slavery, doing away with the last vestiges of Spanish power by his support of a strong army and navy which conquered the Castillo de San Juan de Ulúa, reducing civil and religious holidays, and celebrating for the first time the anniversary of the Grito de Dolores on September 16, 1825, which had been uttered by the martyred Hidalgo.[1]

The President was accused of losing interest in the government once had had achieved his goal as chief executive of the nation. These accusations of indolence and ineptitude were false, Ramirez avers, "for his ardency and unselfishness of ambition for total power have been misinterpreted as disinterest. The real problem lay in the difficulty and turbulence caused by establishing an unfamiliar liberal government which was a drastic change from the despotism and anarchy which prevailed in the past."[2]

The accusation of being "torpid, irresolute, dilatory and jealous of men of ability" is repeated by Parkes,[3] probably based on the attitudes of Alamán and Bustamante. Little credit is given to Victoria for his humanistic traits, his love of liberty for all and his self-sacrifice in the service to his country as expressed by Zavala.[4]

Victoria was vigorous in his activities in setting up a new government for Mexico and in aiding in solving problems for the emerging nation. As a member of the formative Executive Power Committee he showed his awareness of the difficulties facing the new government and made moves to care for the veterans of the war for independence, reestablished discipline in the army and the government, and started public work projects to reconstruct the ravished nation. He set up relations with Colombia, Great Britain, the United States and effected a conciliation with the Vatican. He arranged for the organization of the National Museum and ordered the building of a new school of medicine at the University. Surely these were not activities of an "uncouth barbarian" as Alamán so often referred to him. Further evidence of his ability is found in his encouragement of foreign capital investment to replace that lost by the expulsion of the Spaniards. With the aid of the ever-critical Alamán, the President set up mining corporations to deal with foreign investors under the control of various governmental agencies including: La Anglo Mexicana, La Unida de las Minas de Mexico, and La de Minas de Real del Monto. The first three years of Victoria's reign were successful and followed his ideology of respect and adherence to the laws, obedience and submission to the new constitution and acceptance of the authority of the Congress.[5]

Other worthwhile accomplishments under his regime were new laws pertaining to agriculture and setting up a school for Indian youth at the Colegio de Santa Gregario. President Victoria labored successfully under many difficulties to bring the country out of financial disaster toward a workable economic recovery.

On the first anniversary of the celebration of the Grito de Dolores on September 16, 1825 he proclaimed the freedom of a number of slaves. Some had been given direct freedom by their masters and others had been ransomed through a voluntary collection of funds. On this occasion he said: "On this day in which we celebrate the anniversary of our liberty, let me say that you shall receive in the name of the country, the agreement that there shall be liberty for all, which shall be honored and defended."[6]

His regime was benevolent and the peasants respected the interest he showed in their welfare, but he was severely criticized by those who manipulated him for their own power, especially when he resisted some of their plans. Poinsett was chief among those who, by adroit flattery, won many concessions giving positive power to the United States in trade and property. Among these was a treaty signed on January 12, 1828, and later ratified on April 5, 1832, which settled the boundary question between the United States and Mexico.[7]

Foreign travelers and diarists in Mexico at this period of the new republic varied a great deal in their opinion of the President. Some praised him while others were as violent in their dislike as was Alamán. Edward Thorton Tayloe, a young member of Poinsett's staff, was very critical of Victoria. Tayloe in his journals seldom wrote a kind word about the President. In letters to his family his remarks were scathing and faultfinding of both the national leader and the government. On August 15, 1825 he wrote to his brother, Benjamin: "The government of Mexico, I regret to say, is a feeble one. The President is, I dare say and sincerely hope, conscientiously upright, but his talents are feeble, his health bad, and he is in entire submission to his advisors."[8]

Tayloe was unaware of the strong religious fervor of the Mexicans and was very disparaging of their beliefs. He denounced the Congress for honoring a newly canonized saint, Felipe de Jesus, and castigated the President for walking in a procession honoring the saint who had been martyred in the Philippines by the Japanese.[9]

The young diplomat wrote of Poinsett's activities in establishing lodges of the Yorkinos and of the influences of these lodge groups on the elections and politicians of Mexico. He was amazed that the "Yorkinos, by which this party now dominates, presenting in a Catholic and fanatical country, the curious spectacle of two great parties, which derive their names from orders of Masonry, which the Mexicans have been taught by the priests to believe to be inimical to their religion."[10]

R. W. H. Hardy, a Royal Navy Lieutenant who traveled in Mexico during the term of Victoria describes his first meeting with the President: "This gentleman is of ordinary stature, and whether it was from his bad state of health, or the cloak he wore, I know not, his appearance did not convey the idea, that he possessed that high military feeling and energy which should belong to a man who had been placed by the suffrage of a whole nation in so exalted a position. He received us, however, with courtesy, read my letters, and expressed the current compliments of the country."[11]

Hardy goes on to tell of his experiences in the country and of the many delays he had in trying to deal successfully with various officials. He stated he approached Victoria with his problems and that within fifteen minutes the President had cleared his business activities for a license to seek pearls, which he had requested.[12] Yet, before he left Mexico Hardy became very disgusted with the government of Mexico and its officials. He wrote: "Congress, judges, magistrates, ecclesiastics and military sold themselves for their own individual advantage, and to effect the ruin of their country by making the executive absolute, with a view to their encouraging mischief and promoting faction. The contents of the treasury have been squandered by many of these who had management of national funds, and pillaged by others."[13]

He despaired of trusting anyone and felt that espionage was rampant over the nation. He even lost faith in Victoria, feeling that he too contributed to looting the Treasury: "When Guadalupe Victoria was elected President of the United States of Mexico, he claimed 14,000 dollars of the General Congress as a remuneration for the services he had rendered to the cause of liberty during the time he passed in solitary meditation in a cavern within the state of Vera Cruz. And this sum he obtained."[14] This statement was the only one in which any of the writers of the time mentioned that Victoria received this remuneration. No mention of this payment is made in other documents or books consulted.

In his book on Mexican liberalism, Charles A. Hale refers to Victoria's government as one of coalition and the President as well-meaning, but naively believing that Mexico was destined to unlimited progress and peace. He quotes José María Luis Mora, the ex-cleric liberal, as saying that the question of expulsion of the Spanish, the growing power of the Masons, and Victoria's inability to reconcile the various factions in the country were the chief causes of collapse of the Mexican government in the last years of the 1820s.[15]

Flaccus in his study of Victoria indicates that the Englishmen who had much contact with him--Ward and Pakenham--accused Victoria of being lethargic, stubborn, vain and a showman but also points out that some of these activities might have been due to Victoria's illness which could probably have been hypoglycemia, or a disorder which results in dizziness, fatigue, anxiety, a rapid heartbeat and constant hunger.[16] Considering the years Victoria spent compaing out in the open countryside, living on all types of unorthodox foods and being exposed to the vicissitudes of the tropical weather, it would not be surprising that he had malaria and other tropical diseases which could account for some of his attitudes and health problems. The hypoglycemia theory could account for the psychological signs of anxiety and nervousness. Since there is no medical history available during these years, no definite statements can be verified. When the President died and an autopsy was performed the diagnosis was epilepsy and hypertrophy (enlargement of the heart).[17]

During his years in office Victoria did take an active part in all aspects of governmental activity and worked many long hours. Like any of our disabled American presidents, the health problems of Victoria could have been the seat of some of his erratic activities. Since there are not records of medical diagnostics available for that period of time, the truth of Victoria's ailments--mental or physical--will never be fully revealed unless additional documentation can be located which appears unlikely after 150 years.

8. This statue of Guadalupe Victoria was formerly located in the city of Durango, Durango Province, Mexico. It was moved to Guadalupe Victoria, about forty kilometers east of Durango. Photo by the author.

9. This monument was erected in honor of Guadalupe Victoria in the city of Durango, Durango Province, Mexico in 1954 replacing the one on the opposite page. Details on the erection of the monument are found on the plaque pictured on the following page. Photo by the author.

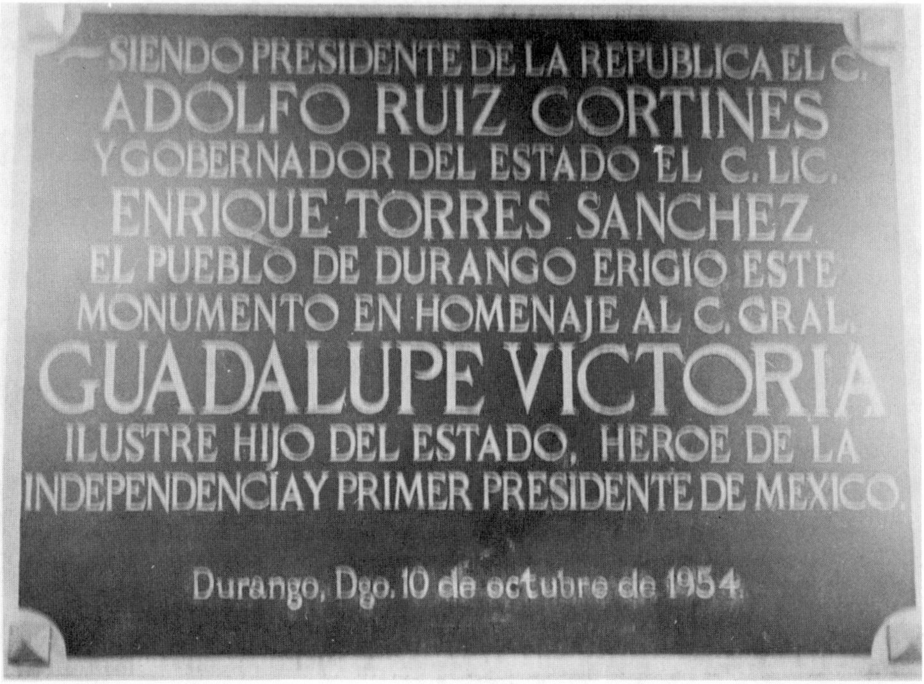

10. Plaque in the interior of the base of the statue shown on the preceding page in honor of Guadalupe Victoria. Photo by the author.

In the golden years of the Victoria regime the faith of the President in his beloved United States of Mexico was supreme. However, being a romantic and a dreamer with high ideals in many ways did not prepare him for the intrigues of his fellow political leaders. Little did he realize when he spoke to the combined chambers on the first of January 1825 of the wonders of independence and the birth of the new nation that the despotisms of the Spanish regime would be transferred to the political leaders of the new republic; that the words he spoke regarding the merit and virtues of the Constitutional Congress would be subdivided by petty jealousies and fights for power by the Centralists and the Liberals; and that the liberty he sought for all under the banner of the Supreme Arbitrator would be ignored for personal gain.[18]

CHAPTER SEVEN

THE DECLINING YEARS

Don Guadalupe Victoria retired to a location in the province of Veracruz, near Tlapacayan, referred to as "El Jobo." The farm, or finca, as it was called, belonged to a group of missionaries from the Philippines, but he was given title to this land in November 1833 partially through purchase and gift. The farm was not a thriving one, in part due to the fact that the general was not capable of managing it adequately because of his continued army assignments and because he was not overly endowed with funds to make necessary improvements.

The government called him in 1833 and 1834 to quell uprisings in Oaxaca and Orizaba. He was active in keeping peace in Puebla and Veracruz and was the negotiator with France in 1838 as well as peacemaker in the uprising at Papantla in 1837. After that time he had few commissions and stayed at "El Jobo."

According to Michael P. Costeloe, Don Guadalupe Victoria, like any other citizen, asked for a loan from the Roman Catholic Church through its lending office, the Juzado de Capellanias.[1] He had asked for his loan prior to the end of his term of office in 1829. After investigation of his personal worth, an allocation of 40,000 pesos was granted to him on June 2, 1829. The guarantor for the loan was José Ignacio Esteva, formerly the Minister of Treasury in Victoria's administration.[2] Although the loan had been approved, money was scarce and by 1831 the ex-president had been granted only the sum of about 16,000 pesos. On this amount he paid interest at the rate of 300 pesos a month.

As the years passed Esteva died, and although a new guarantor was usually required, in Victoria's case it was waived. In 1837 the interest on the property lapsed, but no action was taken to repossess until the general's death in 1843. No information was found as to why he allowed the payments to lapse. Even José de Arrillago, who was appointed by the Juzado to investigate the problem, couldn't make a reasonable report as he found Victoria's papers in an inauditable order. Even as late as 1861 the financial problems of the estate had not been cleared up.

Guadalupe Victoria had planned to use the monies

11. The Finca "El Jobo," in Tlapacoyan, Veracruz, Mexico, the home of the retired general from 1830 until shortly before his death in 1843. This is a view of the courtyard. Photo by the author, 1974.

from the loan to improve the vanilla crop and other agricultural products, but no records were located as to the use the ex-warrior actually made of the funds. Costeloe writes, "Evidently the ambitious development plan envisaged by Victoria ended in ruin and the agriculture of the region deteriorated rather than improved."[3] So ended in disaster another of the veteran insurgent's dreams.

According to Frances Calderon de la Barca, Victoria was still active as Commandante General of the province of Veracruz when she accompanied her husband to Mexico early in 1839. She implied that Victoria was unmarried at that time but was desirous of attaining the married state. She gives a rather unflattering portrait of the general. Her journal states:

> Calderon called this morning on General Victoria. Found his excellency in a large hall without furniture or ornaments of any sort, without even chairs, and altogether in a style of more than republican simplicity. He has just returned the visit, accompanied by his colossal aide-de-camp.

12. Details of the church at "El Jobo," Tlapacoyan, Veracruz, Mexico, which is attached to the hacienda. The church was dedicated to San Jacinto, who was considered the patron of the finca. Photo by the author, 1974.

General Guadalupe Victoria is perhaps the last man in a crowd whom one would fix upon as being the owner of the above high-sounding cognomen, which in fact is not his original, but his assumed name, Guadalupe being adopted in honour of the renowned image of that name, and Victoria with less humility to commemorate his success in battle. He is an honest, down-looking citizen, lame and tall, somewhat at a loss for conversation, apparently amiable and good-natured, but certainly neither courtier nor orator; a man of undeniable bravery, capable of

> supporting almost incredible hardships, humane, and who had always proved himself a sincere lover of what he considered liberty, without ever being actuated by ambition or interested motives.[4]

There is very little documentation on the marital status of Victoria, although Felipe Victoria Gómez says the general had been married to a Doña Felipa Meza who died leaving several offspring.[5] Evidently Mrs. Calderon de la Barca was right when she said that Victoria would like to be married, for shortly afterward the general wrote to Don José María Bretón, father of Doña María Antonia Bretón de los Herreros and asked permission to marry "Tonchita," as he referred to her in a letter written on September 7, 1839.[6]

The general had known Doña Antonia when in Huamantla and had often visited her. With the consent of her father, and, although aware of Victoria's various infirmities, the young woman accepted the proposal. After the wedding the couple lived at the hacienda "El Jobo" and, according to Marquez Montiel, "there she lived a life of tranquility and self-denial."[7] Additional evidence of this marriage is contained in extensive correspondence undertaken by Victoria with various army authorities in 1841 to verify his marriage, presumably so that any benefits accruing to him could be claimed by his wife in case of need.[8]

Ranch life was very difficult and although Victoria spent more time at the hacienda and the adjacent lands that he owned near Nautla and Tecolutla, his exploitation of the property did not produce as many crops as he had hoped and his success was limited. He continued his efforts to improve the land until 1841 when he became seriously ill. Shortly afterward he received a visit from Santa Anna who was appalled at the infirmity of the insurgent general. He called in a military medical consultant, Doctor Antonio del Castillo, who recommended that Victoria spend some time in the more moderate climate of Teziutlán. However, the ex-president's condition did not improve and in the last quarter of the year 1842 he was moved at Santa Anna's request to the military hospital at the Fortaleza San Carlos at Perote.[9] The ex-president did not respond to treatments received and died on March 21, 1843 at 12:30 P.M.

The first president's body was embalmed by the director of the military hospital and buried in the fortress vault, where it remained until it was moved to Puebla in 1863 by General Alejandro Garcia. In 1925 it was finally laid to rest in the Column of Independence on the Paseo de la Reforma in Mexico City along with other heroes of the Republic.

Santa Anna asked for Victoria's name to be inscribed

13. The Fortaleza de Perote, now a military college, located on the outskirts of Perote, Veracruz Province, Mexico. Location of the hospital in which Guadalupe Victoria died in 1843. Photo by the author.

upon a tablet of honor and a monument be erected in his honor at Santa Paula, but his suggestion was not carried out.[10] However, he was declared "Benermérito de la Patria" by the Congress on August 25, 1843. He has been honored by having several city streets, cities and monuments erected in his behalf in recent years.

A rather gruesome anecdote is told about Victoria's remains that Gómez declares is false,[11] but the narrative does add some interesting comments to the legend of Victoria. Marquez Montiel gives this version: "The viscera of Victoria had been placed in a jar of zinc filled with alcohol. During the Mexican-American war some Yankee soldiers found the jar and thirstily drank the alcohol and died shortly thereafter."[12] Several tales and legends surrounding the life of Victoria have been discounted as fantasy for they lack documentation, and this particular event is strongly discounted by Gómez.

As has been mentioned earlier, Victoria was an active campaigner for Mexico and took part in quelling the rebellion of Arista and Duran in 1833,[13] as well as defeating Bravo, who had returned from exile and had again become a problem to the government, which had declared him an outlaw and traitor in 1834. A report from Victoria to the Secretary of War and Navy tells

14. The Column of Independence, Paseo de la Reforma, Mexico City. Photograph reproduced from _México en seis siglos de evolucion_, with permission from the Mexican Consulate, Albuquerque, New Mexico.

about his pursuit of Bravo, and how his troops overwhelmed the enemy, inflicting casualties, killing and dispersing of over one hundred of the enemy.[14]

In 1838 Victoria was one of the two commissioners selected to deal with the French after there were some differences between the two countries that resulted in France overcoming the Castillo de San Juan de Ulúa and defeating Santa Anna in battle in Veracruz where the latter was injured resulting in the loss of his leg.

The French were seeking 600,000 pesos in reparations for loss of goods in the sack of the Parian in 1828 as well as diplomatic settlement of a presumed insult to a Frenchman which led to what has been referred to as the "Pastry War." The French felt that the Mexican government was trying to slight the French and they pressed their claims with a strong military pressure. Negotiations were conducted in which the French Admiral Charles Baudin was reported as being strongly impressed by the straightforwardness and good sense of the former President of the Mexican nation.[15]

Shortly after these negotiations, Victoria called on Santa Anna. Crawford tells of this meeting, in the words of Santa Anna: "Sixty-two days after my foot had been amputated, General Guadalupe Victoria called on me at the instigation of the government. He informed me that a revolution was threatening and that the government desired me to take Bustamante's place as temporary president in these times of trial. . . ."[16]

One of the last public acts that Victoria undertook as a governmental representative was the meeting with Calderón as mentioned earlier. It was quite apparent even at this time that the veteran leader was ailing and having difficulty with epilepsy and lameness from the wounds he had received in battle.

This extraordinary patriot had devoted most of his life from 1811 to 1839 in the service of his government. He had faced all types of hazards, hardships and criticisms, but until the final moments of his death had endured steadfastly all obstacles in the pursuit of freedom for his country.

Waddy Thompson, at one time Envoy Extraordinary and Minister Plenipotentiary from the United States to Mexico, wrote of Victoria in his journals giving a short resume of Victoria's life in which he compared the guerrilla leader to a character worthy of the pages of Plutarch, and lauded him for his consistent loyalty to his country.[17]

Thompson's discourse on Victoria ends with this tribute: "Wherever and whenever that banner [of freedom] was raised, without calculating the chance of success or the consequences of failure, this brave and virtuous man, with a romantic devotion to the liberty of his country, never hesitated in his course. The crowning glory of his life is that he died so poor that he was buried at public expense, and this after filling the highest office of his country, where the facilities of peculations are infinite, and the practice of it much too common."[18]

Even Bustamante, who was requested to do a necrology on Guadalupe Victoria, surprisingly enough gave tribute to him and compared his ardor in obtaining freedom for Mexico to that of the great South American patriot, Simon Bolivar. He goes into detail about Victoria's character: "a slender, well-built man, he was amiable, jovial and loved by the multitudes, especially the negroes of the coast. . . . He was never cruel nor sanguinary but had a compassionate heart and was constant in sustaining the cause of liberty. . . . He gave his heart and sword ardently in combat and was forgiving of his enemies, but was never able to give to his country the peace he desired for it."[19]

GUADALUPE VICTORIA[20]

En el asalto que dieron
á la ciudad de Oaxaca
las huestes, que el gran Morelos
en persona cómandaba,
se registró un hecho heróico,
hecho digno de la fama,
que en bronces debía esculpirse
cual galardón de la patria;
pues sólo en la angigua Roma
se vieron tales hazañas,
por hombres singularísimos
que en su historia se destacan.
Las trincheras de las calles
y los fuertes de la plaza
habían sido ya tomados
á vivo fuego y matanza.
Los repiques de los templos
y las belicosas dianas
resonando por doquiera
la victoria proclamaban;
mas "El juego de Pelota,"
que fortificado estaba
era el teatro de una lucha
sin ejemplo, denodada.
Ancho foso le circuía,
y nadie se aventuraba
á cruzarlo, sin que al punto
en él la muerte encontrara.
Don Guadalupe Victoria
era quien acaudillaba
á los bravos asaltantes
de aquella última muralla

defendida por "realistas,"
y anheloso por tomarla,
en un esfuerzo supremo
de valor, tomó su espada
y arrojándola hasta el muro,
"Allá va en prendas esa arma;"
les gritó con voz tonante,
"voy por ella"; y á la charca
del zanjón echóse á nado,
desafiando la metralla.
Tras él, sus fieles soldados,
victoreándolo, se lanzan
como alud que se despeña;
cual turbión que se desata;
y al desvanecerse el humo
de la contienda empeñada,
la bandera de los libres
ondéo triunfante en la escarpa.

Rafael Del Castillo
Monterrey, Julio 2 de 1910

APPENDIX ONE

Guadalupe Victoria served as President of the Republic of Mexico from October 10, 1824 until March 31, 1829. During his term of office the following men served in his cabinet.

Relaciones Interiores y Exteriores

Juan Guzmán	October 10, 1824--January 11, 1825
Lucas Alamán	January 12, 1824--September 26, 1825
Manuel Gómez Pedraza	September 27, 1825--November 2, 1825
Sebastian Camacho	November 3, 1825--July 5, 1826
Juan J. Espinosa de los Monteros	July 6, 1826--March 7, 1828
Juan de Dios Cañedo	March 8, 1828--January 25, 1829
José María de Bocanegra	January 26, 1829--March 31, 1829

Justicia

Pablo de la Llave	October 10, 1824--November 29, 1825
Miguel Rámos Arizpe	November 30, 1825--March 7, 1828
Juan J. Espinosa de los Monteros	March 8, 1828--March 31, 1829

Guerra y Marina

Manuel de Mier y Terán	October 10, 1824--December 18, 1824
José Castro	December 19, 1824--January 7, 1825
Manuel Gómez Pedraza	January 8, 1825--June 7, 1825
José Ignacio Esteva	June 8, 1825--July 14, 1825
Manuel Gómez Pedraza	July 15, 1825--February 9, 1827

Manuel Rincón	February 10, 1827--March 3, 1827
Manuel Gómez Pedraza	March 4, 1827--December 3, 1828
José Castro	December 4, 1828--December 7, 1828
Vicente Guerrero	December 8, 1828--December 25, 1828
Francisco Moctezuma	December 26, 1828--March 31, 1829

Hacienda

José Ignacio Esteva	October 10, 1824--September 26, 1825
Pablo de la Llave	September 27, 1825--November 27, 1825
José Ignacio Esteva	November 28, 1825--March 4, 1827
Tomás Salgado	March 5, 1827--November 13, 1827
Francisco Garcia	November 2, 1827--February 15, 1828
José Ignacio Pavón	February 16, 1828--March 7, 1828
José Ignacio Esteva	March 8, 1828--January 12, 1829
Bernardo González Angulo	January 13, 1829--March 31, 1829

APPENDIX TWO

This duplicate of a letter written to Pope Leo XIII by Guadalupe Victoria was obtained through the courtesy of Ms. Laura Guiterrez-Witt, Librarian, Latin American Collection of the University of Texas Library and reproduced here with full permission of that institution.

17-5

PRIMERA SECRETARIA

DE ESTADO

Seccion de Estado.

[illegible]

Palacio Nacional. Mexico 27. de Octubre de 1824.

[illegible] 27 de Octubre de 1824

Santisimo Padre.

La Nacion mexicana que cifra su mayor ventura, y felicidad en profesar la Religion Catolica, Apostolica Romana, como la unica verdadera, y capaz de proporcionarle los bienes á que aspira, ha cuidado siempre de mantener su pureza, y de que se conserve intacta, caminando de acuerdo con las potestades Eclesiasticas, sin que en esta parte encontrase contradiccion alguna el Gobierno Español á que estubo sugeta por el espacio de tres siglos.

La gloriosa voz de independencia pronunciada

el año de diez votaron sobre estos principios saludables, concordes con el voto uniforme de la Nacion. y al repetirse el año de veinte y uno se asentó como una de sus bases fundamentales que la Religion Catolica, Apostolica, Romana, seria la de estos payses: con esto no se hizo otra cosa que seguir la voluntad general y acomodarse á los principios unanimemente adoptados.

Verificada la independencia de la antigua España, organizado el gobierno, instalado el primer Congreso Constituyente, derrocado el tirano que por pocos meses oprimió á la Nacion, y restablecido un Sistema de Administracion publica mas analogo al voto y á las necesidades de los pueblos, siempre se ha visto que la Religion traida por los Varones Apostolicos que acompañaron á los Corteses y á los Pizarros, ha sido declarada la dominante del Estado, y la unica cuyo ejercicio permite y protege.

Consecuente á estas ideas cuya universalidad, y certeza comprueban las leyes constitucionales y otros actos solemnes, y privados, uno de los mas ardientes deseos que nos ha ocupado, desde que fuimos colocados al frente de la administracion de los negocios publicos, ha sido el ponernos en comunicacion directa con la Santa Sede, manifestarle nuestros sentimientos, y protestarle á nombre de esta misma Nacion que regimos, aquella obediencia que le es debida como cabeza visible de la Iglesia; pero el trastorno de cosas, inevitables en toda variacion de gobierno, y mucho mas cuando un pais deja de ser Colonia para constituirse en Nacion independiente, ha retardado un paso por que tanto hemos anhelado, y esta demora, no ha sido el menor de los cuidados que ha manifestado á este Supremo Gobierno en medio de los grandes y delicados negocios que se nos han encomendado.

Desde luego hubieramos nombrado un Enviado cerca de esa Corte, revestido de un caracter publico en uso de las facultades que nos estan delegadas por la ley fundamental, con el fin de transmitir los deseos que animan á la Nacion mexicana, y á sus Supremos Poderes; mas la marcha de los negocios publicos suele no ser tan expedita, ni con aquella rapidez que se apetece. No obstante insistimos en nuestras miras religiosas creemos que sin embargo de que muy pronto se verificará la ida del Enviado, es de nuestro deber felicitar á Vuestra Beatitud por su exaltacion á la Silla de San Pedro.

En este feliz acontecimiento vemos renacer los venturosos dias de los Benedictos, Clementes, Pios, y de tantos otros Pontifices que han sido el ornamento de la Iglesia. Nos congratulamos con ella del acierto del Conclave en su ultima eleccion, pues en ella nos há dado un Vicario de Cristo, bajo cuyos auspicios aumentará su brillo, y esplendor la Religion Catolica, Apostolica Romana; y nuestros deseos serán cumplidamente satisfechos si Vuestra Santidad admite benigno estas demostraciones del zelo piadoso que nos anima por el engrandecimiento de la Iglesia.

Las virtudes sublimes que forman el alto caracter de Vuestra Beatitud son el mejor presagio que pueden apetecer los fieles, y ellas anuncian que su repado será feliz y glorioso. Ciertos en este Concepto nos apresuramos á mandar se publicase en todos los lugares de esta República la noticia del ascenso de Vuestra Beatitud al Trono de Roma, al mismo tiempo, que la del restablecimiento de su interesante salud, y nos complacemos en que los Pueblos todos hayan demostrado á porfia el contento y jubilo, que es inherente á una Nacion que hace alarde de ser Catolica.

Tales pues son las ideas de que estamos poseidos como miembros del Poder Ejecutivo que ejercemos, tales los que nos animan como funcionarios encargados del alto Gobierno y tales los sentimientos de toda la Republica mexicana, que hoy está á nuestra direccion. Sirvase pues Vuestra Beatitud de aceptarlos, recibiendo en el entretanto este signo del omenage que le debemos, y de que le somos deudores como á digno sucesor de San Pedro.

Duplicado.

Santisimo Padre

Guadalupe
Victoria

NOTES

Chapter One

1. México. Legislatura. Chamber de Diputados. Derechos del Pueblo Mexicano. México a traves de sus Constituciones. Tomo I, Historia Constitucional 1812-1842 (México: México. XLVI. Legislatura de la Camara de Diputados, 1967), p. 78, pp. 384-385.
2. Richard Eugene Bailey, French Culture in Mexico in the Nineteenth Century (Paris: Boivan, 1936. Thesis, University of Dijon), p. 13.
3. Mark Beaufoy, Mexican Illustrations, founded upon facts; indicative of the present condition of society, manners, religion, and morals, among the Spanish and native inhabitants of Mexico; with observations upon the government and resources of the republic of Mexico, as they appeared during part of the years 1825, 1826, 1827 . . . (London: Carpenter and Son, 1828), p. 82.
4. Diego Garcia Loya, Mosaic of Mexican History (México, D. F.: Editorial Cultura, T. G., S. A., 1958, 1960), p. 143.
5. Ibid., p. 144.
6. Ibid., p. 145.

Chapter Two

1. José Fernándo Ramírez, Noticias históricos y estadísticas de Durango . . . 1849-1850 (México, D.F.: Cumplido, 1851), p. 74.
2. Spain. Archivo de las Indias. Audencia. Seccion Quinta, 1814.
3. Felipe Victoria Gómez, Guadalupe Victoria, Primer Presidente de México. Biografía Documentada (Mexico, D.F.: Ediciones Botas, 1952), p. 11. See also: Eduardo Enrique Ríos, Robinson y su adventura en México (Figuras y Episodios de la Historia de México, n. 61. México: Editorial Jus, 1962), p. 264.
4. Ramírez, Noticias históricos, p. 83.
5. Ramírez, ibid., p. 85.
6. Gómez, Guadalupe Victoria, pp. 11-12.
7. José María Cos y Perez was invaluable as a surgeon to the rebels but also as an outstanding spokesman for the insurgency cause. In an early period when the

Spaniards had feared for their safety in Zacatecas, they had sent out Dr. Cos as an intermediary, and he was touched when they received him with great courtesy. This impressed him and later when they related their case, he became sympathetic and lauded their cause. Viceroy Francisco Javier Venegas made overtures to him, as did General Calleja, to retain his support, but he eventually joined the insurgents. Dr. Cos is best known for his Plan de Paz y Plan de Guerra as well as his publication of the periodical, Ilustrador Nacional and his writing of El Despertador Americano, and for his membership in the rebel congress established in 1813. He accepted the indulto in 1817, resided in Pátzcuaro where he practiced medicine until his death in 1819.

8. José María Luis Mora, Méjico y Sus Revoluciones (Paris: Librería de Rosa, 1856), vol. 4, pp. 395-400. Additional detail is also available in Heriberto Frías, Episódios Militares Mexicanos . . . . (Paris y México: Librería de la Vda. de Ch. Bouret, 1901), pp. 252ff.

9. Gamaliel Arenas, Guadalupe Victoria o Sea Don Manuel Félix Fernández, Campeon y Héroe de la Independencia y Primer Presidente de la Republica. A fragment of a book, n.p., n.d.

10. Lucas Alamán, Historica de Méjico desde los Primeros Movimientos que Preparon su Independencia en el Año 1808, hasta la Época Presenta (México: Editorial Jus, 1942), v. 3, pp. 320-324, 329. See also: Loya, Mosaic of Mexican History, pp. 168ff; and Manuel Rivera Cambas, Los Gobernantes de México. Galería de Biografías y Retratos de los Vireyes, Emperadores, Presidentes y Otras Gobernantes que Has Tenido México, desde Don Hernando Cortés hasta el c. Benito Juarez (México: Impresa Imp. de J. M. Aguilar Ortiz, 1873), vol. 2, p. 111.

11. Gómez, Guadalupe Victoria, p. 8.

12. Ramírez, Noticias Históricos, p. 73-74. See also: Frances Erskine (Inglis) Calderón de la Barca, Life In Mexico During A Residence Of Two Years In That Country; with a preface by W. H. Prescott (London: Chapman and Hall, 1843), p. 58ff.

13. Lucas Alamán, Historia de Méjico, vol. 3, pp. 301-302. For more details see also: Niceto de Zamacois, Historia de Méjico Desde Sus Tiempos Más Remotos . . . (México: J. F. Parres y Cia., Barcelona-México, 1879-1882), vol. 8, pp. 656-657.

14. Loya, Mosaic of Mexican History, p. 167.

15. Fayette Robinson, Mexico and Her Military Chieftains, from the Revolution of Hidalgo to the Present Time . . . (Hartford, Conn.: Silas Andrus and Son, 1851), p. 50.

16. Loya, Mosaic of Mexican History, p. 168. See

also: Alberto Bremauntz, Panorama Social de las Revoluciones de México (México: Ediciones Jurídico Sociales, 1960), p. 83.

17. Loya, Mosaic of Mexican History, p. 170.

18. Josiah Conder, The Modern Traveller . . . (Boston: Wells, Lilly and Thomas Wardle, 1830), p. 107.

19. México. Legislature. Camara de Diputados, Derechos del Pueblo Mexicano. México a Traves de Sus Constituciones, Historia Constitucional, 1812 - 1843 (Mexico: SLVI Legislatura de la Camara del Diputados, 1967), vol. 1, pp. 41-42, 80-81.

20. Manuel Garcia Puron, México y Sus Gobernantes: Biografías (México: Libreria de Manuel Porrúa, S. A., 5 de Mayo 1949), pp. 142-145.

21. Archivo General de Indias. Sevilla, Spain. Audencia de México. Seccion Quinta, v. 1482, Estante 90, Cajon 1, Legajo 19. Félix María Calleja al Ministro de Gracia y Justicia (México: 18 Agosto de 1814). For English translation see Ward, Mexico in 1827, Appendix, vol. 1, pp. 509-525.

22. Fayette Robinson, Mexico and Her Military Chieftains, pp. 54-55.

23. Brantz Mayer, Mexico: Aztech, Spanish and Republican; A Historical, Geographical, Political, Statistical and Social Account of That Country from the Period of the Invasion by the Spaniards to the Present Time . . . (Hartford: S. Drake and Company, 1851), vol. 1, pp. 291-292.

24. Juan E. Hernández y Dávolos, Colección de Documentos para la Historia de la Guerra de Independencia de México de 1808 a 1821 . . . . (México: J. M. Sandoval, 1878-1882), vol. 5, p. 214, numero 91.

25. Francisco Bulnes, La Guerra de Independencia: Hidalgo--Iturbide . . . . (México: Editorial Nacional, 1965, vol. 1, p. 324.

26. Lorenzo de Zavala, Ensayo Histórico de las Revoluciones de México desde 1808 hasta 1820 . . . . (Paris: Imp. de P. Dupont et G. Laguionie [etc.] 1831-32, vol. 1, p. 324.

27. México. Legislatura. Camara de Diputados, Derechos del Pueblo Mexicano, vol. 1, pp. 376ff.

28. Hubert H. Bancroft, History of Mexico (San Francisco, California: A. D. Bancroft & Company, Publishers, 1885), vol. 4, p. 617.

29. Beaufoy, Mexican Illustrations, p. 88.

30. Beaufoy, ibid., pp. 88-89. A literal translation. For another interpretation see: Heriberto Frías, Episódios Militares Mexicanos. Principales Campañas, Jornadas, Batallas, Combates y Actos Heroicos Que Ilustran la Historia del Ejército Nacional desde la Independencia hasta el Triunfo Definitivo de la República. Primero Parte. Guerra de Independencia. (Paris y México: Librería de la Vda. de Ch. Bouret, 1901), Appendix XII, pp. 404-405.

31. Justo Sierra, Evolucion Política del Pueblo Mexicano (México: La Casa de España, 2d ed., Sepanola, 1940), p. 179.
32. Ward, Mexico in 1827, vol. 1, p. 210.
33. Alberto Bremauntz, Panorama Social de las Revoluciones de México (México: Ediciones Juridico Sociales, 1960), p. 80.
34. Bremauntz, ibid., p. 81.
35. México. Legislatura. Camara de Diputados, Derechos del Pueblo Mexicano, vol. 1, p. 78.
36. Ibid., p. 79.

Chapter Three

1. J. C. Beltrami, Le Mexique . . . Tome Premier (Paris: Crevot, Delaunay Libraire, 1830), pp. 64-65.
2. Ramírez, Noticias Históricos, p. 74.
3. Ibid., p. 76.
4. Alamán, Historia de Méjico, vol. 4, p. 98.
5. Josep María Miquel i Vergés, La Diplomacia Española en México, 1822-1823 (México: Colegio de México, 1956), p. 72.
6. Francisco de Paula de Arrangoiz y Berzábal, México desde 1808 hasta 1867; prólog de Martin Quirarte (México: Editorial Porrúa, 2d ed., 1968), p. 132.
7. M. S. Alperovich, Historia de la Independencia de México, 1810-1824. Traduccion del ruso de Adolfo Sanchez Vazquez (México: D. F., Editorial Grijalbo, S. A., 1967), p. 192.
8. Alamán, Historia de Méjico, vol. 4, pp. 215, 230.
9. Bancroft, History of Mexico, vol. 4, p. 640.
10. Alperovich, Historia de la Independencia de México, p. 192.
11. Alamán, Historia de Méjico, vol. 4, p. 98; Gómez, Guadalupe Victoria, pp. 27-31.
12. Bancroft, History of Mexico, vol. 4, p. 629.
13. Alamán, Historia de Méjico, vol. 4, p. 221.
14. Bancroft, History of Mexico, vol. 4, p. 630.
15. Mariano Cueves, S. J., Historia de la Nacion Mexicana . . . (México: Talleras Tipografícos Modelo, S. A., 1940), pp. 350ff.
16. Fayette Robinson, Mexico and Her Military Chieftains, pp. 63-64.
17. Ward, Mexico in 1827, p. 226; Alamán, Historia de Méjico, vol. 4, pp. 230-231.
18. Herbert Ingram Priestley, The Mexican Nation (New York: Macmillan, 1924), p. 244.
19. Manuel Rivera Cambas, Historia Antigua y Moderna de Jalapa y de las Revoluciones del Estado de Veracruz (México: Imprenta de I. Cumplido, 1869), vol. 2, pp. 26-27.

20. Harris Gaylord Warren, The Sword Was Their Password; a History of American Filibustering in the Mexican Revolution (Baton Rouge, La.: Louisiana State University Press, 1943). Many pages of this book deal with purchases of supplies and munitions by various agents of the Mexican republican government.

21. William Davis Robinson, Memoirs of the Mexican Revolution: Including a Narrative of Expedition of General Xavier Mina. . . . (London: Lackington, Hughes, Harding, Mavor and Lepard, 1821), vol. 1, pp. 232-233. See also: Bancroft, History of Mexico, vol. 4, pp. 634-635, including notes, and Rivera Cambas, Historia Antigua, vol. 2, pp. 31-34.

22. Ibid., p. 233.

23. Mayer, Mexico, p. 294.

24. Yoakum Henderson, ed., Memoir of Ellis P. Bean Written about Himself about the Year 1816 (Austin: Book Club of Texas, 1930), In Bennett Lay, The Lives of Ellis P. Bean (Austin: University of Texas Press, 1960), the name of Bean's wife is given as Doña Magdalena Falfan de los Godos rather than Anna Garthas.

25. Rivera Cambas, Historia Antigua, vol. 1, pp. 61-62.

26. Miquel i Vergés, La Diplomacia Española, p. 11. A detailed account of the Mina expedition is given in William Davis Robinson, Memoirs, vol. 1, pp. 95ff.

27. Rivera Cambas, Historia Antigua, vol. 1, p. 87. See also: Rivera Cambas, Gobernantes, vol. 2, p. 112, and Beaufoy, Mexican Illustrations, p. 85.

28. Ward, Mexico in 1827, vol. 1, p. 230; also Alamán, Historia de Méjico, vol. 4, p. 594ff.

29. Ibid., vol. 1, p. 230. See also: Fayette Robinson, Mexico and Her Military Chieftains, p. 66.

30. Mariano Cuevas, S.J., Historia de la Nacion Mexicana (México: Talleres Tipografícos Modela, S.A., 1940), p. 453.

31. Don Juan Ruiz de Apodaca, Diarias y Correspondencia de Virrey Don Juan Ruiz de Apodaca, 1816-1821. 54 volumes. (Madrid: Real Academia de Historia. Manuscripts with Index). These were examined at random since they were too extensive to cover in depth. These papers contained the names of many of those who accepted the Viceroy's pardon and gave details about expenditures, battles, and details of court life during Apodaca's reign.

32. Bancroft, History of Mexico, vol. 4, p. 694.

33. México Estima a Apodaca Como Verey de la Paz (México: Oficina de D. J. María Benavente y Socios, 1820). A pamphlet written by an anonymous author included in the Archives of Audencia. Seccion Quinta. Sevilla, Spain

Chapter Four

1. W. B. Bullock, Six Months Residence and Travels in Mexico (London: John Murray, 1824), pp. 454-455. See also: Ward, Mexico in 1827, vol. 1, pp. 228-234.
2. Miquel i Vergés, La Diplomacia Española, p. 13.
3. Basil Hall, Extracts from a Journal, Written on the Coasts of Chile, Peru and Mexico in the Years 1820, 1821, 1822 . . . (London: Moxon, 1830), vol. 2, p. 233.
4. Ibid., p. 233. See also: Bancroft, History of Mexico, vol. 4, pp. 704-705.
5. Ward, Mexico in 1827, vol. 1, pp. 525-526. For a detailed description of the Plan of Iguala see: Bustamente, Cuadro Histórico de la Revolucion Mexicana, vol. 5, pp. 112-114.
6. Garcia Puron, México y Sus Gobernantes, pp. 145-146. See also: Beaufoy, Mexican Illustrations, p. 90.
7. Arenas, Guadalupe Victoria, p. 275. See also: Ward, Mexico in 1827, vol. 1, pp. 232-233.
8. Bustamente, Cuadro Histórica, vol. 4, p. 177. Copies of the original proclamation are available in the files of the Hernández y Dávalos collection at the University of Texas and in the Mexican Independence Papers, 1810-1821 in the Clements Library of the University of Michigan.
9. Miquel i Vergés, La Diplomacia Espanol, p. 73.
10. William Spence Robertson, Iturbide of Mexico (Durham, N.C.: Duke University Press, 1952), p. 94. See also: Zavala, Ensayo Histórico, pp. 114-115; Cuevas, El Libertador, p. 67.
11. Hall, Extracts from a Journal, pp. 240ff.
12. México. Chapultepec Castle. Museo de Historia. Documentos de Independencia (México, 1821). A broadside.
13. Garcia Puron, México y Sus Gobernantes, p. 149.
14. Hall, Extracts from a Journal, p. 243.
15. Alperovich, Historia de la Independencia de México, p. 218.
16. Bustamente, Cuadro Histórico, vol. 4, pp. 18-19.
17. Cuevas, El Libertador, pp. 66-67.
18. Hall, Extracts from a Journal, p. 244.
19. Muñoz, Antonio López de Santa Anna, p. 37.
20. Ibid., p. 31. See also: Callcott, Santa Anna, p. 37.
21. Bullock, Six Months Residence, p. 454.
22. Frank Cleary Hanighen, Santa Anna, The Napoleon of the West (New York: Coward-McCann, 1934), p. 26.
23. (Guadalupe Victoria), Plan ó Indicaciones para Reintegrar a la Nacion en sus Naturales, e Imprescrip-

tibles Derechas y Verdadera Libertad, de todo lo que se Haya con Escandolo de los Pueblos Cultos Violentamente Despajada per D. Agustín de Iturbide, siendo esta Medida de tan Estrema Necesidad, qu sin ella Es Imposible el que la America del Septentrion Pueda Disfrutar enlo venidero una Paz Salida y Permanente (Veracruz: Imprenta de Priani y Socio, 6 December 1822).

24. William Spence Robertson, Iturbide of Mexico, p. 24. See also: (Guadalupe Victoria), Choque de don Victoria y el brigadier Santana, Acabado con Balazos (México: Imprenta de Ontineros, 1822). This is a discussion on the conspiracy of Lemaur and Santana and of the intrigues and ambitions of Santana.

25. Muñoz, Antonio López de Santa Anna, pp. 51-52. All historians of the period concur on the accuracy of this event.

26. Ibid., pp. 54-55.

27. México. Secretarío del Supremo Poder Ejectivo. Borrador de Carta al General Guadalupe sobre la Embarcacion de Iturbide (México: May 2, 1823).

28. Zavala, Ensayo Histórico, p. 188.

29. Rivera Cambas, Gobernantes, p. 113.

30. Miquel i Vergés, La Diplomacia, pp. 78-79. Details on this series of meetings can be found in: Guadalupe Victoria, Gobierno de Nueva Espana. Oficio que el Escmo. Sr. Secretario de Estado y Relacio Interiores y Estoriores (Habana: Imprenta Fraternal de las Diaz de Castro, Impresores del Consulado, y del Ayuntamiento por S. M., 1823).

31. Ibid., p. 145.

32. Ibid., p. 146.

33. Bullock, Six Months Residence, p. 453. For more information about British influence in Mexico at this time please consult: J. Fred Rippy, Historical Revolution of Hispanic America (New York: Crofts, 1922), pp. 375ff; and Luis Chávez Orozco, Historia de México 1808-1836 (México: Editorial Patria, 1947), vol. 1, pp. 186-187.

34. Mariano Cuevas, Historia de la Nacion Mexicana . . . (México: Talleres Tipografícos Modelo, S. A., 1940), p. 499.

35. Bancroft, History of Mexico, vol. 5, p. 15.

36. Chávez Orozco, Historia de Mexico, pp. 242ff.

37. Bremauntz, Panorama Social de las Revoluciones de México, p. 88.

Chapter Five

1. México. Legislacion Mexicana. Coleccion Completa de las Disposiciones Legislativas Expedidas Desde la Independencia de la República; Ordenada por los Licenciados Manual Dublan y José María Lozano. Edicion

Oficial. (México: Imprenta del Comercio, 1876), vol. 1, p. 719 (No. 426).

2. Rivera Cambas, Gobernantes, p. 114.

3. México. Presidente. Informes y Manifestos de los Poderes Ejecutivo y Legislativo de 1821 á 1904. . . Publicacion Hecha por J. A. Castillon de Orden del Señor Ministro de Gobernacion Don Ramón Corrall . . . . Tomo. I. (México: Imprenta del Gobierno Federal, 1905), pp. 28-29.

4. Hanighen, Santa Anna, pp. 31-32.

5. John Frost, The History of Mexico and Its Wars. . . . (New Orleans: Armand Hawkins, 1882), p. 165.

6. Beaufoy, Mexican Illustrations, p. 110.

7. México. Presidente. Los Presidentes de México ante la Nacion; Informes y Documentos de 1821 a 1966. Editado por XLVI Legislatura de la Camara de Diputados (México, 1966).

8. U.S. National Archives, National Archives and Records Service, Notes from the Mexican Legation in the United States to the Department of State, 1821-1906. Microcopy No. 54, Roll 1, Vols. 1-2, November 30, 1821 --December 11, 1835. (Washington: General Services Administration, 1960) Letter dated August 30, 1824.

9. México. Presidente. Informes y Manifiestos, pp. 36-39.

10. Chávez Orozco, Historia de México, pp. 244-245.

11. Callcott, Church and State, p. 56. Justo Sierra in his interpretation of events in México, Su Evolucion Social, trans. by G. Sentiñon (México: J. Ballesca and Co., 1900), pp. 176ff of vol. 1, implies that Poinsett was very influential in setting up the lodges in Mexico.

12. Arrangoiz y Berzábal, Mexico desde 1808 hasta 1867, vol. 2, pp. 173-174.

13. Richard E. Greenleaf, "The Mexican Inquisition and the Masonic Movement, 1751-1820," New Mexico Historical Review 44:2, 1969, pp. 94-117. See also: Sierra, Evolucion Politica del Pueblo Mexicano, vol. 1, p. 156. He says that the army was completely undermined by free-masonry imported by the French with a tremendous spirit of proselytism.

14. Bremauntz, Panorama Social, p. 89.

15. Cuevas, S.J., Historia de la Nación Mexicana . . . (México: Talleras Tipografícos Model, S. A., 1940), pp. 522-523.

16. Ibid., p. 524.

17. José Fuentas Mares, Poinsett; Historia de una Grand Intriga. 2d ed. (México: Jus, 1958), pp. 18-19.

18. Bustamente, Voz de la Patria, vol. 2, no. 15, p. 8.

19. Henry Bamford Parkes, History of Mexico, rev. and enl. (Boston: Houghton, Mifflin Company, 1950), p. 191.

20. William R. Manning, Diplomatic Correspondence of the United States Concerning the Independence of Latin-American Nations, selected and arranged by William R. Manning (New York: Oxford University Press, 1925), vol. 3, p. 1636-, doc. no. 893.

21. An interesting sideline in this trading was discovered in one case found in the Bernardo Bourdin Papers in the University of Texas Bexar Archives containing a number of letters written by Bernard Bourdin, a citizen of New Orleans represented by Joaquin Bulnes. He was attempting to get 17,424 pesos with six percent interest for munitions and supplies sent to Generals Anaya and Guadalupe Victoria in 1816. The case continued for a period of twenty-five years. Appeals had been made to Victoria in 1840 and 1842 to intercede with the government to make payment to the Bourdin heirs. Victoria did so several times, but no payment had been made as late as 1843. Bernardo Bourdin, Papers, 1827-1850, 1 vol. (Austin: University of Texas Library, Texas Archives).

22. Callcott, Santa Anna, p. 54. See also: Sierra, Evolución del Pueblo Mexicana. 2d ed. (México: Esposa, 1940), p. 215.

23. Bremauntz, Panorama Social, pp. 79, 85-86.

24. Beaufoy, Mexican Illustrations, p. 24.

25. Alamán, Historia de Méjico, vol. 5, p. 810.

26. Bancroft, History of Mexico, vol. 5, pp. 37-40.

27. Hanighen, Santa Anna, p. 32.

28. Please see Appendix One for full listing of names of the men that held the various positions.

29. Sierra, México, Su Revolución Social, vol. 1, pp. 177ff.

30. Beaufoy, Mexican Illustrations, p. 107.

31. Bancroft, History of Mexico, vol. 5, p. 43.

32. Chávez Orozco, Historia de Mexico, vol. 1, pp. 262-263. See also: M. Apologia de Victoria en los Dias de La Acordada o Sean Varias Refleciones Sobre el Estado de La República (México: Imprenta del C. Rafael Nunez, 1829). An eight-page pamphlet in the British Museum.

Chapter Six

1. México (D.F.), Direccion de Acción Cívica de Reforma y Cultura, D. Guadalupe Victoria (México, D.F.: Su Propaganda Cívica, no. 64, 1929). 2 pages.

2. Ramírez, Noticias Históricos, pp. 84-85.

3. Parkes, History of Mexico, p. 188.

4. Zavala, Ensáyo Histórico, p. 192. See also: Alfonso Teja Sabre, Guide to the History of Mexiço (México: Press of the Ministry of Foreign Affairs, 1935), p. 290.

5. México. El Supremo Poder Ejecutivo a la Nacion, Manifesto del Supremo Poder Ejecutivo de la Republica Mexicana, a los Habitantes de sus Estados Federados (México: Imprenta Nacional del Supremo Gobierno, en Palacio, 1824). 6 pages.

6. Francisco Sosa, Biografías de Mexicanas Distinguidas (México: Oficina Tipografíca de las Secretaria de Fomento, 1884), p. 1075. See also: Rivera Cambas, Gobernantes, pp. 116-128.

7. Treaties and Other International Agreements of the United States of America, 1776-1949; compiled under the direction of Charles I. Bevans (Washington: Department of State, U.S. Government Printing Office, 1968), vol. 9, p. 760.

8. Edward Thorton Tayloe, Mexico, 1825-1828; the Journal and Correspondence of Edward Thorton Tayloe, ed. by C. Harvey Gardiner (Chapel Hill, N.C.: The University of North Carolina Press, 1959), p. 72.

9. Ibid., pp. 113-114.

10. Ibid., pp. 89, 113-114.

11. R. W. H. Hardy, Travels in the Interior of Mexico in 1825, 1826, 1827 and 1828 (London: Henry Colburn and Richard Bentley, 1829), p. 10.

12. Ibid., p. 22.

13. Ibid., p. 528.

14. Ibid., p. 518.

15. Charles A. Hale, Mexican Liberalism in the Age of Mora, 1821-1853 (New Haven: Yale University Press, 1968), p. 115.

16. Elmer W. Flaccus, "Guadalupe Victoria: His Personality as a Cause of His Failure," The Americas, vol. 23, no. 3, January 19, 1967, pp. 297-311.

17. México. Secretaría de Guerra y Marina. Colección de Documentos Históricos Mexicanos; formada por orden del c. Subsecretario de Guerra y Marina con Acuerdo del c. Presidente Constitucional de la Republica (Paris and México: Librería Vda. de Ch. Bouret, 1920), vol. 1, pp. 107-111.

18. México. Presidente. Informes y Manifiestos de los Poderes Ejecutivo y Legislativo de 1821 á 1904 (México: Imprenta del Gobierno Federal, Tomo I, 1905), pp. 37-39.

Chapter Seven

1. Michael P. Costeloe, "Guadalupe Victoria and a Personal Loan from the Church in Independent Mexico," The Americas, vol. 25, no. 3, January 1969, pp. 223-224.

2. Ibid., p. 225.
3. Ibid., p. 239.
4. Frances Erskine (Inglis) Calderón de la Barca, Life in Mexico During a Residence of Two Years in That Country; with a preface by W. H. Prescott (London: Chapman and Hall, 1843), pp. 23-24.
5. Gómez, Guadalupe Victoria, p. 179.
6. Joaquín Marquez Montiel, Datos Raros Sobre Caudillos de la Independencia (Coleccion Heroica, 21. México: Editorial Jus, 1963), pp. 70-71.
7. Ibid., p. 71.
8. México. Secretaría de Guerra y Marina. Colección de Documentos Históricos Mexicanos (Tomo Primero. Librería de la Vda. de Ch. Bouret, 1920), p. 62.
9. Ibid., p. 63.
10. Rivera Cambas, Gobernantes, p. 130.
11. Gómez, Guadalupe Victoria, p. 179.
12. Marquez Montiel, Datos Raros Sobre Caudillas, pp. 72-73.
13. Agustín Guiol, Estraordinaria de la Sedducion al General Victoria (México: Impresa en las Escalerillas, por al Ciudadano Agustín Guiol, 1833). 1-page broadside in the British Museum. See also: Guadalupe Victoria, Proclama del General Guadalupe Victoria, Commandante General del Estado de Pueblo, a las Tropas de Su Mondo (México: Imprenta de la Libertad a Cargo del c. Cosme Guerra, 1833). 1-page broadside in the British Museum.
14. Guadalupe Victoria, Estraordinaria, Derrota y Fuga del Traidor Ex-General Bravo (México: Impreso por Juan Ojeda, Puente de Palacio y Flamen--cos numero 1, Enero 17 de 1834). 1-page broadside in the British Museum.
15. Eugéne Maissin, The French in Mexico and Texas, 1838-1839, translated from the French with introduction and notes by James L. Shepherd, III (Salado, Texas: A. Jones Press, 1961), p. 93.
16. Ann Fears Crawford, ed., The Eagle; the Autobiography of Santa Anna (Austin: The Pemberton Press, 1967), p. 65.
17. Waddy Thompson, Recollections of Mexico (New York: Wiley and Putnam, 1846), p. 62.
18. Ibid., p. 62.
19. Carlos María Bustamente, Necrologia. El Gral. D. Guadalupe Victoria (México: Biblioteca Nacional, S.P.L., 8 p.). A bound pamphlet containing clippings taken from the periodical El Siglo 19, n.d.
20. Taken from Manuel Acuña, Vicente Riva Palacio, José Rosas Moreno, et al., Romancero de la Guerra de Independencia . . ., ed. by De Victoriano Agueros, Tomo II (México: Imprenta de "El Tiempo," 1910).

BIBLIOGRAPHY

BOOKS, MEMOIRS AND DIARIES

Alamán, Lucas. História de Méjico desde los Primeros Movimientos que Prepararon Su Independencia en el Año de 1808 Hasta la Época Presente. México: Editorial Jus, 1942. 5 v.

Alessio Robles, Vito. Coahuila y Texas; desde la Consumacion de la Independencia Hasta el Tratado de Paz de Guadalupe Hidalgo. Tomo Primero. México, 1945.

--------. Mier Noriega y Guerre, José Servando Teresa de, 1765-1827. El Pensamiente del Padre Mier. Nota biografica y seleccion de Vito Alessio Robles. Bibliografia Enciclopedia Popular, No. 16. México; Septiembre, 1944.

Alperovich, M S., Historia de la Independencia de México, 1810-1824. Traduccion del Ruso de Adolfo Sanchez Vazquez. México: Editorial Grijalbo, S. A., 1967.

Apodaca, Don Juan Ruiz de. Diarias y Correspondencia de Virrey Don Juan Ruiz de Apodaca, 1816-1821. Madrid, Spain: Real Academia de História. 54 v.

Arenas, Gamaliel. Guadalupe Victoria ó Sea Don Manuel Félix Fernández, Campeon y Heroe de la Independencia, y Primer Presidente de la Republica. Fragment of a book. n.p., n.d.

Arrangoiz, Francisco de Paula de. México Desde 1808 Hasta 1867. Prólogo de Martin Quirarte. 2d. ed. México: Editorial Porrua, 1968.

Bailey, Richard Eugéne. French Culture in Mexico in the Nineteenth Century. Paris: Boivan, 1936. Thesis, University of Dijon.

Bancroft, Hubert Howe. History of Mexico. San Francisco: A. D. Bancroft and Company, 1883-1888. 6 v.

Barker, Eugene C. Mexico and Texas, 1821-1835. University of Texas Lectures on the causes of the Texas Revolution. Dallas, Texas: P. L. Turner Company, 1928.

Beaufoy, Mark. Mexican Illustrations, Founded Upon Facts; Indicative of the Present Condition of Society, Manners, Religion, and Morals, Among the Spanish and Native Inhabitants of Mexico: With Observations Upon the Government and Resources of the Republic of Mexico, As They Appeared During

Part of the Years 1825, 1826, and 1827. . . . London: Carpenter and Son, 1828.

Beltrami, J C. Le Mexique. . . . Tome Premier. Paris: Crevot, Delaunay, Libraire, 1830.

Benson, Nettie Lee. La Diputación Provincial Y el Federalismo Mexicano. México, D.F.: El Colegio de México, 1955.

Betancourt, Salvador L. Album Histórico Mexicano. S. L. Betancourt y A. Sodi, Editores. [México, 1923].

Bocanegra, José María. Memorias Para la Historia de México Independiente, 1822-1846. México: Imprenta del Gobierno, 1892-1897. 2 v.

Bremauntz, Alberto. Panorama Social de las Revoluciones de México. México: Ediciones Juridico Sociales, 1960.

Bullock, W. Six Months' Residence and Travels in Mexico Containing Remarks on the Present State of New Spain; Its Natural Productions, State of Society, Manufacture, Trade, Agriculture, and Antiquities. . . . With Plates and Maps. London: John Murray, 1824.

Bulnes, Francisco, La Guerra de Independencia: Hidalgo-Iturbide. . . . México: Editorial Nacional, 1965. 2 v.

Bustamante, Carlos María. Cuadro Histórico de la Revolución Mexicana Comenzada en 15 de Septiembre de 1810. . . . 2d. ed. Corr. México, D.F.: Tallares Linotipograficas, Soria, 1026. 5 v.

--------. Continuación del Cuadro Históricos de la Revolución Mexicana. México: Publicaciones de la Biblioteca Nacional de México, 1953. 2 v. in 1.

--------. Necrologia. El Gral. D. Guadalupe Victoria. 8 pages of clippings from the periodical El Siglo XIX.

--------. Resúmen Histórica de La Revolución de los Estados Unidos Mejicanos. . . . por D. Pablo de Mendibil. Londres: La Publica R. Ackerman . . ., 1828.

Calderon de la Barca, Madame Frances Erskine (Inglis). Life in Mexico During a Residence of Two Years in That Country. Preface by W. H. Prescott. London: Chapman and Hall, 1843.

--------. Life in Mexico. The letters of Fanny Calderón de la Barca; with new material from the Author's Private Journals. Edited and annotated by Howard T. Fisher and Marion Hall Fisher. New York: Doubleday and Comapny, Inc., 1966.

Callcott, Wilfried Hardy. Church and State in Mexico, 1822-1857. New York: Columbia University, 1926. Ph.D. dissertation.

--------. Santa Anna: The Story of an Enigma Who Once Was Mexico. Hamden, Conn.: Archon Books, 1964.

Caruso, John Anthony. The Liberators of Mexico. New York: Pageant Press, 1954.

Castillo Negrete, Emilio del. México en el Siglo XIX O Sea Historia Desde 1800. . . . México: Imprenta en las Escalerillas, etc. 1875-1892. v. 5 only one used.

Chávarri, Juan N. Historia de la Guerra de Independencia de 1810-a-1821. En Commemoración al 150 Aniversario. México: Editorial Latino Americano, 1960.

--------. Las Hombres de la Independencia. Trienta Biografías. México: Libro Mexicana, Editores, 1958.

Chávez Orozco, Luis, Historia de México, 1808-1836. México: Editorial Patria, 1947.

El Comercio Exterior y La Expulsión de los Españoles. Introducción por Luis Chavez Orozco. Colección de Documentos Para la Historia del Comercio Exterior de México, 2. Series 2. México: Banco Nacional del Comercio Exterior, 1966.

Conder, Josiah. The Modern Traveller; a Popular Description, Geographical, Historical, and Topographical of Mexico and Guatimala. Boston: Wells, Lilly and Thomas Wardle, 1830.

Crawford, Ann Fears, Editor. The Eagle; the Autobiography of Santa Anna. Austin, Texas: The Pemberton Press, 1967.

Cuevas, Luis Gonzago. Porvenir de México; Introducción de Francisco Cuevas Cancino. México: Editorial Jus, 1954.

Cuevas, Mariano, S.J. Historia de la Nación Mexicana. . . . México: Talleres Tipografícos Modela, S.A., 1940.

--------. El Libertador. Documentos Selectos de D. Agustin de Iturbide. México: Editorial Patria, 1947.

Delgado, Jaime. España y Mexico en el Siglo XIX. Apendice Documental, 1820-1845. Instituto Gonzalo Fernández de Oviedo. Madrid: Consejo Superior de Investigaciones Cientidias, 1950.

Diccionario Porrúa de Historia. Biografía y Geografía de Mexico. 2d. ed. México: Librería de Porrúa Hermanos y Cia, 1946.

Estep, Raymond. Lorenzo de Zavalla: Profeta del Liberalismo Mexicano. Traduccion de Carlos A. Echaveve Trujillo. Prólogo de Carlos E. Castañeda. México: Librería de Manuel Porrúa, 5 de Mayo, 1949.

Episodios Históricos de la Guerra de Independencia Relatados por Varios Autores. . . . México: Agueros, 1910. 2 v. in 1.

Flaccus, Elmer W. Guadalupe Victoria: Mexican Revolutionary Patriot and First President, 1786-1843. Texas: University of Texas, 1951. Ph.D. dissertation.

Frías, Heriberto. Episódios Militares Mexicanos. Principales Campañas, Jornadas, Batallas, Combates y Actos Heroicos Que Ilustran la Historia del Ejército Nacional Desde la Independencia Hasta el Triunfo Definitivo de la República. Primero Parte. Guerra de Independencia. Paris y México: Librería de la Vda. de Ch. Bouret, 1901.

Frost, John. The History of Mexico and Its Wars. . . . New Orleans, La.: Armand Hawkins, 1882.

Fuentas Mares, José. Santa Anna: Aurora y Ocaso de un Comediante. 2d. ed. Figuras y Episodios de la Historia de Mexico, 73. México: Editorial Jus, 1959.

--------. Poinsett: Historia de una Gran Intriga. 2d. ed. Figuras y Episodios de la Historia de Mexico, 51. Includes Bibliografía. México: Editorial Jus, 1958.

Galindo, Dr. Miguel. El Mito de la Patria. . . . Colima: 1920.

García, Genera. Documentos Inéditos ó Muy Raros Para a la Historia de México. Noticias bio-bibliografícas de Alumnos Distinguidos de Colegio de San Pedro, San Pablo y San Ildefonso de México . . ., por el Dr. Félix Osores, Segunde y Ultima Parte. México: Librería de la Vda. de Ch. Bouret, 1908. v. 21.

Garcia Puron, Manuel. México y Sus Gobernantes: Biografías. México: Librería de Manuel Porrúa, S.A., 5 de Mayo 1949.

Gómez, Felipe Victoria. Guadalupe Victoria, Primer Presidente de México. México: Botas, 1952.

Gonzalez de Cossio, Francisco. Xalapa; Breve Reseña Historico. México: 1957.

Gregory, Samuel. Gregory's History of Mexico. . . . Microfilm, Travel Literature, Reel 9; no. 118. Originally published in 1847.

Guiol, Augustín. Estraordinaria de la Sedducion al General Victoria. México: Impresa en las Escalerillas, por al Ciudadano Agustín Guiol, 1933.

Gutiérrez de Lara, Lazaro. The Mexican People: Their Struggle for Freedom. By L. Gutiérrez de Lara . . . and Edgcumb Pinchon. Illustrated from photographs. Garden City, New York: Doubleday, Page & Company, 1914.

Hall, Basil. Extracts from a Journal, Written on the Coasts of Chile, Peru and Mexico in the Years 1820, 1821, 1822. . . . London: Moxon, 1840. 2 v. in 1.

Hanighen, Frank Cleary. Santa Anna. The Napoleon of the West. New York: Coward-McCann, 1934.

Hardy, R W H (Lieut.) Royal Navy. Travels in the Interior of Mexico in 1825, 1826, 1827, and 1828. London: Henry Colburn and Richard Bentley, 1829.

Hernández y Dávolos, Juan E. Colección de Documentos Para la Historia de la Guerra de Independencia de

México de 1808 a 1821. Biblioteca de "El Sistema Postal de la Republica Mexicoana." México: J. M. Sandoval, 1878-1882. 6 v. Used v. 4 exclusively.

Junco, Alfonso. Un Siglo de Mejico, de Hidalgo a Carranza. 4h. ed. Madrid: Ediciones Cultura Hispanica, 1956.

Lay, Bennett. The Lives of Ellis P. Bean. Austin, Texas: University of Texas Press, 1960.

Liceago, José María de. Adiciones y Rectificaciones a la Historia de México que Escribo D. Lucas Alámam, formadas y Publicadas. Guanajuato: Empreso de E. Serrano, 1868.

Logan, Walter Seth. The Siege of Cuautla, The Bunker Hill of Mexico. New York: The Knickerbocker Press, 1893.

Loya, Diego Garcia. Mosaic of Mexican History. México, D.F.: Editorial Cultura, T.G., S.A., 1958, 1960.

Magner, James Aloysius. Men of Mexico. Milwaukee: Bruce Publishing Company, 1942.

Maissin, Eugene. The French in Mexico and Texas (1838-1839). Translated from the French with introduction and notes by James L. Shepherd, III. Salado, Texas: The Anson Jones Press, 1961.

Manning, William R. Diplomatic Correspondence of the United States Concerning the Independence of the Latin-American Nations. Selected and arranged by William R. Manning . . . New York: Oxford University Press, 1925. Used v. 3 only.

Marquez Montiel, Joaquín. Datos Raros Sobre Caudillos de la Independencia. Coleccion Heroica, 21. México: Editorial Jus, 1963.

Mayer, Brantz. Mexico: Aztech, Spanish and Republican; a Historical, Geographical, Political, Statistical and Social Account of That Country from the Period of the Invasion by Spaniards to the Present Time. . . . Hartford: S. Drake and Company, 1851. v. 1.

México, Secretaría de Educación Pública. México y la Cultura. México: Secretaría de Educación Pública, 1946.

México en Seis Siglos de Evolucion. n.p., 1925.

México y las Colonias Extranjeras en el Centenario de la Independencia, 1810-1910. [México, 1910].

Mier Noriega y Guerra, José Servando Teresa de. Memoria polítical-instructiva, enviada desde Filadelfia en Agosto de 1821, a los gefes independientes del Anahuac, llamado por los Españoles Nueva España. Impresa en Filadelfia y reimpresa en México, en la Oficiana de M. Ontiveros, 1822.

Miquel i Vergés, José María. Diccionario de Insurgentes. México: Editorial Porrúa, S.A., 1969.

--------. La Diplomacia Española in México, 1822-23. 1st. ed. México: Colegio de México, 1956.

Mora, José María Luis. Méjico y Sus Revoluciones. Paris: Librería de Rosa, 1856. 4 v.

Morales Diaz, Carlos. Quien es Quien en la Nomenclatura de la Cuidad de México. México: Impresora Barrie, 1962.

Muñoz, Rafael F. Antonio López de Santa Anna. Edicion Completa Según el Texto Original. México: 1937.

Navarrete, Félix. La Masonería en la Historia y en las Leyes de Méjico. México: Editorial Jus, S.A., 1957.

Nicholson, Irene. The Liberators; a Study of Independence Movements in Spanish America. New York: Praeger, 1969.

Palacios, Enrique Juan. Puebla: Su Territorio y Sus Inhabitantes. México: Departmento de Talleres Graficas de la Secretaria de Fomento, 1917.

Parkes, Henry Banford. A History of Mexico. Boston: Houghton Mifflin, 1970. Sentry edition, with illustrations.

Poinsett, Joel R. Notes on Mexico, Made in the Autumn of 1822. Accompanied by an Historical Sketch of the Revolution, and Translations of the Official Reports on the Present State of That Country. London: J. Miller, 1825.

Quirarte, Martin. Vision Panoramica de la Historia de México. 2d. ed. México: 1966.

Ramírez, José Fernándo. Noticias Históricos y Estadísticas de Durango. . . . (1849-1850). 2d. ed., 1910. México: Imprenta de Ignacio Cumplido, 1851.

Read, Benjamin Maurice. Illustrated History of New Mexico. Santa Fe: 1912.

Ríos, Eduardo Enrique. Robinson y Su Adventura en México. Figuras y Episodios de la Historio de México, 61. México: Editorial Jus, 1962.

--------. El Historiador Davis Robinson y Su Aventura en Nueva España. México: Antigua Librería Robredo, de José Porrúa e Hijos, 1939.

Rippy, J. Fred. Historical Revolution of Hispanic America. New York: Crofts, 1933.

Riva Palacio, Vicente, Editor. México á Través de los Siglos. Barcelona: Espasa y Companía, 1888-1889. 5 v.

Rivera Cambas, Manuel. Los Gobernantes de México. Galería Biografías y Retratos de los Vireyes, Emperadores, Presidentes y Otras Gobernantes que Has Tenido México, Desde Don Hernando Cortés Hasta el c. Benito Juarez. México: Imprenta de J. M. Aguilar Ortiz, 1873. v. 2 only.

--------. Historia Antigua y Moderna de Jalapa y de las Revoluciones del Estado de Veracruz. 3 Tomos. México: Imprenta de I. Cumplido, 1869.

Rives, George Lockhart. The United States and Mexico, 1821-1848. New York: Charles Scribner's Sons, 1913. v. 1.

Robertson, William Spence. Hispanic-American Relations

with the United States. Edited by David Kinley. New York: Oxford University Press, 1923.
--------. Iturbide of Mexico. Durham, N.C.: Duke University Press, 1952.
Robinson, Fayette. Mexico and Her Military Chieftains, from the Revolution of Hidalgo to the Present Time, Comprising Sketches of the Lives of Hidalgo, Morelos, Iturbide, Santa Anna, Gómez Farias, Bustamento, Paredes, Almonte, Arista, Alamán, Ampudia, Herrera, and De La Vega. Hartford, Conn.: Silas Andrus and Son, 1851.
Robinson, William Davis. Memoirs of the Mexican Revolution. Including a Narrative of the Expedition of General Xavier Mina. To Which Are Annexed Some Observations on the Practicability of Opening a Commerce Between the Pacific and Atlantic Oceans, Through the Mexican Isthmus, in the Lake of Nicarague; and the Vast Importance of Such Commerce to the Civilized World. London: Lackington, Hughes, 1821.
Rouaix, Pastor. Diccionario Geografía, Historia y Biografía del Estado de Durango. México: IPGH, 1946.
Sierra, Justo. Evolución Política del Pueblo Mexicano. 2d. ed. México: La Casa de España, Sepanola, 1940.
--------, Editor. México, Su Evolucion Social. Translated by G. Sentiñon. México: J. Ballesca and Co., 1900. 3 v.
Sosa, Francisco. Biografías de Mexicanos Distinguidos. México: Oficina Tipografíco de la Secretaria de Fomento, 1884.
--------. Las Estatuas de la Reforma. Noticias biografías de los Personajes en Ellas Representados. 2d. ed. México: Oficina Tipografíco de la Secretaria de Fomento, 1900.
Sprague, William F. Vicente Guerrero, Mexican Liberator, A Study in Patriotism. Chicago: Donnelly and Sons, 1939.
Tamaron y Romeral, Pedro. Demostración del Vastisimo Obispado de la Nueva Vizcaya--1765. Durango, Sinaloa, Sonora, Arizona, Nuevo Mexico, Chihuahua y Porciones de Texas, Coahuila y Zacatecas. Con una Introducción Bibliográfica y Acotaciones por Vito Alessio Robles. Biblioteca Histórica Mexicana de Obras Ineditas, no. 7. México: Angigua Librería Robredo, de José Porrúa e Hijos, 1937.
Tayloe, Edward Thornton. Mexico, 1825-1828. The Journal and Correspondence of Edward Thornton Tayloe. Edited by C. Harvey Gardiner. Chapel Hill, North Carolina: The University of North Carolina Press, 1959.
Teja Zabre, Alfonso. Guide to the History of Mexico. Mexico: Press of the Ministry of Foreign Affairs, 1935.

Thompson, Waddy. Recollections of Mexico; by Waddy Thompson, Esq., Late Envoy Extraordinary and Minister Plenipotentiary of the United States At Mexico. New York and London: Wiley and Putnam, 1846.

Timmons, Wilbert H. Morelos of Mexico: Priest, Soldier, Statesman. El Paso, Texas: Texas Western College, 1963.

Tornel y Mendívil, José María. Breve Reseña Histórica de los Acontecimientos Más Notables de la Nación Mexicana, desde el Año 1821 Hasta Nuestras Días. . . . Edicion de la Ilustracion Mexicana. México: Imprenta de Cumplido, 1852.

Toro, Alfonso. Compendio de Historia de México; La Revolución de Independencia y México Independiente. . . . Quinta Edicion. Corregida y Aumentada con Bibliográfias, Mapas e Ilustraciones Documentales. Obra Premiada con Medalla de Ora en La Exposicion Ibero-Americana de Sevilla. México: Editorial Patria, S.A., 1947.

Torres Quintero, Gregoria. La Patria Mexicana; Elementos de Historia Nacional. . . . Tercer Ciclo; Decimaoctava Edicion. México: E. M. Herrero y Cia., 1947.

Torrente, Mariano. Historia de la Independencia de México. Biblioteca Ayacuch, XXXIII. Madrid: Editorial America, 1918.

Ugarte, José Bravo. Historia de México; Independencia, Caracterizacion Political y Integracion social. México: Editorial Jus, 1944.

United States, Department of State, Washington, D.C. Treaties and Other International Agreements of the United States of America, 1776-1949. Compiled under the direction of Charles I. Bevans. . . . Washington: Department of State, U.S. Government Printing Office, 1968. v. 9.

Valades, José C. Santa Anna y la Guerra de Texas. Segunda Edicion. Muy Aumentada y Corregida. México: Editorial Patria, S.A., 1951; México: Imprenta Mundial, 1936.

Vargas, Fulgencio. El Estado de Guanajuato; Geografía, Estadística e Historia Sinteticas. . . . Contribucion de Gobierno deGuanajuato al Primer Congreso Mexicano de Historia. Guanajuato, Gto., México: Talleres Linotipográficos del Estado, 1933.

Vasconcelos, José (Calderon). Breve Historia de México. Coleccion Hombres e Ideas. Madrid: Ediciones Cultura Hispanica, 1952.

Vasquez Santa Ana, Higinio. Bosquejos Biografícos de Hombres Ilustres Nacionales. México: Secretaria de Gobernacion Direccion de Talleres Graficos, 1920.

Villaseñor y Villaseñor, Alejandro, . . . Obras del

Lic. Villaseñor y Villaseñor. . . . México: Imprenta de V. Agueros, 1897-1910. vols. 7, 57, 73.
--------. Biografías de los Héroes y Caudillos de la Independencia. Coleccion México Héroico, no. 11. México: Editorial Jus, 1962. v. 2.
Ward, Sir Henry George, Esq. Mexico in 1827. His Majesty's Chargé de Affairs in That Country During the Years, 1825, 1826, and During Part of 1827. London: Henry Colburn, 1828.
Warren, Harris Gaylord. The Sword Was Their Passport; a History of American Filibustering in the Mexican Revolution. Baton Rouge, La.: Louisiana State University Press, 1943.
Yoakum, Henderson K. History of Texas From Its First Settlement in 1685 to Its Annexation to the United States in 1846. . . . With an Extended Appendix in which are contained the Ellis P. Bean's Memoirs. New York: Redfield, 1856. 2 v.
Zamacois, Niceto de. Historia de Méjico desde Sus Tiempos Más Remotos. . . . México: J. F. Parres y Cia, Barcelona-México, 1879-1882. 18 v.
Zavala, Lorenzo de. Ensayo Histórico de las Revoluciones de México desde 1808 hasta 1830. Paris: Imp. de P. Dupont et G. Lagiuonie (etc.), 1831-32. v. 1.

BIBLIOGRAPHIES

Bibliographic Index. New York: H. W. Wilson Company, 1942. Section on Mexico, subdivision under the period.
California. University. Library. Spain and Spanish America in the Libraries of the University of California. Berkeley, California: University of California Press, 1930.
Carrera Stampa, Manuel C. Archividia Mexicana. México: Instituto de Historia, University Nacional Autonomous de la México, 1952.
Guide to Historical Literature. Editors include: William Henry Allison, Sidney Bradshaw Fay, Augustus Hunt Shearer and Henry Robinson Shipman. New York: Macmillan, 1931. Section Y: Hispanic-American, Mexico, pp. 1076-1080.
Guanajuato, México. Coleccion de Documentos Relativos a la Época de la Independencia de México. Guanajuato, México: A. Chagoyan, 1870.
Guide to the Hispanic American Historical Review, 1918-1945. Edited by Ruth Lapham Butler. Chapel Hill: Duke University Press, 1950.
Jones, C K. A Bibliography of Latin American Bibliographies. 2d. ed. Washington: U.S. Government

Printing Office, 1942. Mexico: pp. 192-240. Catalog: pp. 2024-2495b.

Keniston, Hayward. List of Works for the Study of Hispanic History. New York: Hispanic Society of America, 1920.

México. Biblioteca Nacional. Catalogo Especial de las Obras Mexicanas a Sobre México. México: Imprenta de Arturo Garcia Cubas Sucs, Hnos., 1911.

Millares Carlo, Agustín. Ensayo de Una Bibliografía de Bibliográfias Mexicanas. México: Carlo y José Ignacio Mantecon, 1942.

Palau y Dulcet, Antonio. Manual de Librero Hispano-Americano. Barcelona, 1923-1927.

Texas. University. Library. Independent Mexico in Documents: Independence. Empire. Republic: a Calendar of the Hernández y Dávalos Manuscript Collection. Prepared by Carlos E. Castañeda and Jack A. Dabbs. Mexico: Editorial Jus, 1954.

United States Hispanic Founcation of the Library of Congress. Handbook of Latin American Studies. Edited by Francisco Aguilera. vols. 1-13, 1935-1947. Cambridge: Harvard University Press, 1948.

Spain. Archivo General de las Indias. Seville. Independencia de America: Fuentes Para Su Estudio; Catalogo de Documentos Conservados en el Archivo General de Indias de Sevilla. 1 Series. Madrid: Establishmento Tipografícas de la Sociedad de Publicaciónes Históricos, 1912.

BROADSIDES, PUBLICATIONS AND MANIFESTOS OF GUADALUPE VICTORIA

(Victoria, Guadalupe). Choque de don Guadalupe Victoria y el brigadier Santana, acabado con balazos. México: Imprenta de Ontiveros, 1822. (British Museum.)

(Victoria, Guadalupe). Compatriotas. Espero me Hareis, etc. A manifesto issued on his appointment as a member of the Supremo Poder Ejecutivo, and dated 7 July 1824. 3 pp. México: Imprenta del Supremo Gobierno en Palacio, 1824. (British Museum.)

Victoria, Guadalupe. Derrotero de las Islas Antillas, de las Costas de Tierra Firme, y de las del Seno Mexicano, Corregído y aumentado y con un apéndice sobre las Corrientes del Océano Atlantico á Mandado Reimprimir. Por el Exmo. Sr. D. Guadalupe Victoria. . . . México: 1825. A book on tides and currents of the Atlantic Ocean.

(Victoria, Guadalupe). Estraordinaria. Derrota y Fuga del Traidor Ex-general Bravo. Viva la Federacion! A one-page dispatch written from Campo de Petlama, Enero 14 de 1834 by Guadalupe Victoria to Excamo.

Sr. Ministro de Guerra y Marina. México: Impreso por Juan Ojeda, Puenta de Palacio y Flamenco, Enero 17 de 1834. Cos Número 1. 1 leave. (British Museum.)

(Victoria, Guadalupe). Estraordinario Violento. . . . A military dispatch to the Escmo. Sr. Presidente D. Antonio Lopez de Santa Anna, dated Puebla, Julio 10 de 1833. México: Imprenta del Callojon de Flores letre C, a Cargo del Ciudadino José Guadalupe Anacosta, Julio 11 de 1833. 1 leaf. (British Museum.)

(Victoria, Guadalupe). Gobierno de Nueva España. Oficio que el Escmo. Sr. D. Guadalupe Victoria, desde Jalapa al Escmo. Sr. Secretario de Estado y Relacio Interiores y Estoreriores. Dated: 18 June, 1823. Speaks of the negotiations at Jalapa with the Spanish Commissioners. Habana: Imprenta Fraternal de los Diaz de Castro, impresores del Consulado, y del Ayuntamiento por S.M., 1823. (British Museum.)

Victoria, Guadalupe. Guadalupe Victoria, Comandante general de la Provincia de Veracruz, a los Valientes Defensores de la Independencia Megicana. Compañeros. . . . In which the General speaks of the welfare of the nation and of the necessity of continued vigilance. San Juan del Rio, 16 de Junio de 1821. México: Imprenta Portatil del Egercito de las Tres Garantias, 1821. (British Museum.)

(Victoria, Guadalupe). Noticia Extraordinaris; Sobre la Rendicion de la Capital. A declaration which speaks of the tyranny of Iturbide, need to seek liberty and of the six decrees leading to liberty. Signed by Guadalupe Victoria and many other leaders and deputies. México: Impresa en Veracruz y Reimpresa en México en la Oficina Liberal á Cargo de D. Juan Cabrera, Año de 1823. 4 leaves. (British Museum.)

(Victoria, Guadalupe). Parte Oficial, del Escmo. Sr. General D. Guadalupe Victoria, sobre el alcance de Canalizo y Duran. A letter to the Secretaria de Guerra y Marina about the march against the rebels; and dated: Oajaca, Noviember 11 de 1833. This copy produced in México, Noviembre 16 de 1833 by Ignacio Justiniani. México: Impreso por Juan Ojeda, esquina del Volador y Flamenco, 1833. 1 leaf. (British Museum.)

(Victoria, Guadalupe). Plan ó Indicaciones para Reintegrar a la Nacion en Sus Naturales, ó Imprescriptibles Derechos y Verdadera Libertad, de Todo lo que Se Haya con Escandolo de los Pueblos Cultos Violentamente Despajada per D. Agustin de Iturbide, Siendo Esta Medida de Tan Estrema Necesidad, que sin ella Es Imposible el que la America del Septentrion Pueda Disfrutar en lo Venidero una Paz Solida y Permaente. Outline for a plan to set up a new independent republic. Signed by Guadalupe Victoria and Antonio López de Santa Anna. Copied by Mariano Barbabosa, Secretario. Veracruz: Imprenta de Pirani y Socio, 6 December 1822. 8 pages. (British Museum.)

Victoria, Guadalupe. Proclama. Campo en Santa Fe sobre Veracruz, Spril 20, 1821. 1 leave. HD-14-2.1384. Latin American Collection, University of Texas. Speech given at Santa Fe, near Veracruz, in which he speaks of independence throughout the Americas. (Clements Library, University of Michigan.)

(Victoria, Guadalupe). Proclama de El Ciudadano Guadalupe Victoria, Brigadier de los Exercitor Nacionales, y Comandante Gral. de la Prov. de Veracruz. A plea to the Mexican people to continue fighting on behalf of independence. Signed: José Guadalupe Victoria. n.d. (Clements Library, University of Michigan.)

(Victoria, Guadalupe). Proclama del General Guadalupe Victoria, Commandante General del Estado de Puebla, a las Tropas de su Mando. A speech against tyranny, for a liberty without excesses, declares that Mexico should always be free. Given at Puebla, 12 de Julio de 1833. México: Imprenta de la Libertad a Cargo del c. Cosmo Guerra, 1833. (British Museum.)

(Victoria, Guadalupe). Respuesta: Que Dió del general Victoria al Escelentísimo Ayuntamiento de Veracruz. Praising Veracruz for being the foremost leader in the fight for independence and always identifying itself in seeking sovereignty for the nation. Veracruz: 1822. (Latin American Collection, University of Texas.)

(Victoria, Guadalupe). Tres Palabritas á Victoria y Santana por Varios Amantes de S.M. México: Ontiveros, 1823. 2 pages. A criticism of Iturbide. (British Museum.)

BROADSIDES, PAMPHLETS AND MISCELLANY

Acta de la Junta de Puebla, Sobre la Reinstalacion del Congreso Mexicano; Puebla: 9 Marzo 1823. México: Oficina del Ciudadano Fernández de Lara, 1823. 2 p. In the British Museum: 9770,k.7 (177).

Aunque Se Embarque Iturbide, Ha de Volver los Más Pronto, Si Victoria y el Gobierno No Tomas Sus Precauciones. México: Oficina Liberal, 1823. 2 p. In the Biblioteca Nacional, Mexico City.

La Batalla de D. Guadalupe Victoria con las Tropas de

Veracruz. Signed by Initials: E.A.R.M.D. México: Oficina de D. José María Ramos Palomera, 1822. In the Sutro Library, San Francisco, California.
Defensa del Ciudadano General D. Guadalupe Victoria. Signed by Initials: A.M. México: Oficina de D. José María Ramos Polomera. 16 de Agosto de 1822. 4 p. In the Sutro Library and British Museum, 9770. bb. 11 (3.).
. . . Dos insurgentes: Fray Luis G. Oronoz.--El Br. José M. Correa. Archivo y Biblioteca de la Secretaría de Hacienda. Coleccion de documentos historicos, t.1. México: Tip. de la Oficina impresora de estampillas, 1914.
Estraordinaria de la Seduccion al General Victoria. 7 Julio 1833. México: Impresa en las Escalerillas, por el Ciudando Agustin Guiol, 1833. 5 p. In the British Musuem: 9770.k.11. (65.).
(Gratis) Estraordinario de Puebla; Recibido Hoy 10 de Julio 1833. México: Impreso en las Escalerillas, por el Ciudadano Agustin Guiol, 1833. 1 p.
Gualupe (sic) Victoria: No Quiere Emperador Sino Emperadora. México: Imprenta de D. J. M. Benavenre y Secios, 1823. 4 p. (In the Sutro Library.)
Iturbide, Agustín de. Barrador de Carta a Navarrete. Livorno, Agusto 2, 1823. Unsigned, incomplete. 10 leaves. In Mariano Cuevas, El Libertador. . . . México: Editorial Patria, 1947.
--------. Carta a Nicolás Bravo Nombrando a Pedro del Paso y Troncoso como Apoderado en los Negocios relatios a Su Embarcación. Perote, April 27, 1823. In Mariano Cuevas, El Libertador. . . . México: Editorial Patria, 1947.
López de Santa Ana, Antonio; Guadalupe Victoria; and Mariano Barbosa. Plan de Pronunciamiento en Veracruz y Reforma que se le Hicieron. Veracruz, December 6, 1822. In José María Bocanegra, Memorias Para la Historia de México Independiente, 1822-1846. México: Imprenta del Gobierno, 1892-1897. 2 v.
M. Apologia de Victoria en los Dias de la Acordada. O Sean Varias Reflecsiones Sobre el Estado de la Republica. México: Imprenta del C. Rafael Nuñez, 1829. 8 p. In the British Museum, 8180.f.22.
México Estima a Apodaca Como Virey de la Paz. Initialed "P." México: Oficina de D. J. María Benavente y Socios. 7 p. In the Archivo General de Indias, Sevilla, Spain. R.1036F. IA 11/3 7.
Ramos, José María, et al. Idea de la Conspiracion Descubierta en la Capital del Imperio Mexicano en 26 de Agosto de Este Año. (México): Impersta Imperial y Octubre 15 de 1822.
X.Z. Peticion Pública al Sr. Presidente Contra Sus Ministros. México, Julio 13 de 1826. (México):

Oficina de la Testamentaria de Ontivertos, Año de 1826. 1 p. In the British Museum: 9770,k.9 (17.).

DOCUMENTS

México. Archivo General del Nacion. Papel Varios. Tramo Numbero 1. Secciones numeros: 39, 66, 67, 99, 101, 108, 112, 116, 138, 196.

México. Archivo General del Nacion. Secretaria de Gobernacion. Los Percursores Ideologicos de la Guerra de Independencia. La Masoneria en México, Siglo XVIII. Tomo II. Estados Unidos Mexicanos, Publicaciones del Archivo General de la Nacion, XXI. México: Talleres Graficos de la Nacion, 1932.

México. Archivo General del Nacion. Secretaria de Gobernacion. Documentos para la Historia de la Guerra de Independencia, 1810-1822. Correspondencia Privada de Don Agustín de Iturbide y Otros Documentos de la Epoca. Estados Unidos Mexicanos, Publicaciones del Archivo General de la Nacion, XXIII. Del Archivo del Teniente Coronel Don Manuel de Iruela y Zamora. México: Talleres Graficos de la Nacion, 1933.

México. Archivo General de la Nacion. Seccion de Expulsión de los Españoles y Persecuciones Españoles, 1826-1827. Tramo Numero 1. Secciones numeros: 60, 66, 67.

México. Biblioteca Nacional. Papel Varios. "Proclama del Sr. Coronel D. Antionio López de Santa-Ana a' los habitantes de Veracruz en la ocupación de aquella plaza." Campo de estramuros de Vera Cruz, 27 de Octubre de 1821. Reimpresa en la Oficina de Mariano Ontiveron. México: 1821.

México. Comité Nacional del Comercio. Album Oficial. Ler Centenario del la Independencia de México, 1810-1910. México: Gomez de la Puente, 1910. 1 v.

México. Comité Organizador de la Participación en la Exposición Ibero-Americana de Sevilla. México: Talleres Gráficos de la Nacion, 1929. Luis A. Herrera, Editor; Francisco A. Saenz, Presidente.

México. (D.F.) Dirección de Acción Cívica, de Reforma y Cultural. D. Guadalupe Victoria. Su Propaganda Cívica, no. 64. México, 1929.

México. Laws and Statutes, etc. Derecho Público Mexicano. Compilación continene: Importantes Documentos Relativos a la Independencia. . . . Heca por El Lic. Isidro Antonio Montiel y Duarte en Virtud de orden del c. Ministro de Justicia, Lic. José María Iglesias. Tomo I. México: Imprenta de Gobierno, en Palacio. . . ., 1871.

México. Legislacion Mexicana. Coleccion Completa de

las Disposiciones Legislativas Expedidas Desde la Independencia de la República; Ordenada por los Licenciados Manuel Dublan y José María Lozano. Edicion Oficial. México: Imprenta del Comercio, 1876. v. 1.

México. LXVI Legislatura de la Camara de Deputados. Derechos del Pueblo Mexicano. México a Traves de sus Constituciones. Tomo I. Historia Constitucional, 1812-1842. México: 1967.

México. Ministerio de Guerra y Marina. . . . Colección de Documentos Historicos Mexicanos, Formada por Orden del c. Subsecretario de Guerra y Marina con Acuerdo del c. Presidente Constitucional de la Republica. . . . Paris, México: Librería de la Vda. de C. Bouret, 1920-26. 4 v. in 2.

México. Museo de Historia. Chapultepec Castle. Documentos Ineditos. Regencia: Junta Gubernativa Periodo. México: n.d.

México. Museo de Historia. Chapultepec Castle. Documentos Ineditos. Regencia: Junta Gubernativa Periodo. México: n.d.

México. Presidente. Informes y Manifiestos de los Poderes Ejecutivo Legislativo de 1821 á 1904. . . . Publicación hecha por J. A. Castillon de order del Señor Ministro de Gobernación Don Ramón Corral. . . . Tomo I. México: Imprenta del Gobierno Federal, 1905.

México. Presidente. Manifiesto del Presidente de los Estados-Unidos Mexicanos, a sus compatriotas. México: Imprenta del Supremo Gobierno de las Estados-Unidos Mexicanos, 1824.

México. Presidente. Manifiesto del Supremo Poder Ejecutivo de la Republica Mexicana, a las Habitantes de sus estadas Federales. México: Imprenta Nacional del Suprema Gobierno, 1824.

México. Presidente. Los Presidentes de México ante la Nación; Informes y Documentos de 1821 a 1966. Editado por XLVI Legislatura de la Cámara de Diputados. México: 1966.

México. Secretaría de Guerra y Marina. Colección de Documentos Historicos Mexicanos. Formada por orden del C. Subsecretario de Guerra y Marina con Acuerdo del C. Presidente Constitucional de la Republica. Tomo Primo. Librería de la Vda. de Ch. Bouret. Paris and México: 1920.

México. Secretaría de Guerra y Marina. Colección de Documentos Historicos Mexicanos. Formada por orden del C. General Jefe del Departmento de Justicia, Archivo y Biblioteca Lic. Roberto Lagaray. Tomo Segundo. México: Antigua Imprenta de Murguia, 1924.

México. Secretaría de Hacienda y Credito Publico. Semblanza Historico de Mexico. México: Direccion

General de Prensa, Memoria, Bibliotecas y Publicaciones, 20 Noviembre 1960.

México. Secretaría de la Defensa Nacional. La Correspondencia de Agustín de Iturbide Despues de la Proclamacion del Plan de Iguala. Archivo Histórico Militar Mexicano, N. 1. Con una Advertencia y una Introduccion por Alessio Robles. México: Talleres Autográfico, 1945. 2 v.

México. Secretaría del Supremo Poder Ejectivo. Borrador de Carta al General Guadalupe sobre la Embarcacion de Iturbide. (México: May 2, 1823.)

México. Secretaría de Relaciones Exteriores. La Diplomacia Mexicana; Pequeña Revista Historica. Por Antonio de la Peña y Reyes. . . . Archivo Historico Diplomatico Mexicano, Number I. México: Publicaciones de la Secretaría de Relationes Exteriores, 1923.

México. Secretaría de Relaciones Exteriores. El Congreso de Panamá y Algunos Otros Proyectos de Union Hispano-Americana. Archivo Historico Diplomático Mexicano, Number 19. México: Publicaciones de la Secretaría de Relaciones Exteriores, 1926.

México. Secretaría de Relaciones Exteriores. Las Relaciones Entre México y el Vaticano. Archivo Historico Diplomatico Mexicano, Number 27. México: Publicaciones de la Secretaría de Relaciones Exteriores, 1928.

México. Secretaría de Relaciones Exteriores. Un Esfuerzo de México por La Independencia de Cuba. Con prologo por Luis Chavez Orozco. Archivo Historico Diplomático Mexicano, Number 32. México: Publicaciones de la Secretaría de Relaciones Exteriories, 1930.

México. Secretaría de Relaciones Exteriores. Un Siglo de Relaciones Internacionales de México. A Traves de los Mensajes Presidenciales. Con un prologo por Genaro Estrada, Director del Archivo Historico Diplomático. Archivo Historico Diplomático Mexicano, Numbero 39. México: Secretaría de Relaciones Exteriores, 1935.

México. Universidad Nacional Autonomico de México. Documentos Para la Historia de Mexico: El Supremo Poder Ejecutivo a la Nacion. v. 6. México: 5 de Octubre 1824. UNAM #393. México: Imprenta Nacional del Supremo Gobierno, en Palacia, 1824.

United States National Archives. National Archives and Records Service. Notes from the Mexican Legation in the United States to the Department of State, 1821-1906. National Archives Microfilm Publications, no. 54. Roll 1, vols. 1-2, November 30, 1821--December 11, 1835. Washington: General Services Administration, 1960.

SELECTED LETTERS

Kittera, Thomas. Quarterly Communication to Joel R. Poinsett Extending Permission by Resolution to Grant Warrants of Constitution to Mexican Lodges. Dated 5 June 1826. (From the collection of the Historical Society of Pennsylvania, Philadelphia.)

Noticias de Roma. Carta de nuestro Santísimo Padre el Señor Leon XII al Ecsmo. Sor. Presidente de los Estados Unidos Mexicanos Ciudadano Guadalupe Victoria, Dirigida con Nota del Eminentisimo Señor Cardenal Secretario de estado, al respectivo de la República. Guanajuato, 30 Noviembre de 1825. Reimpreso en la Oficina del Superior Gobierno, a Cargo del C. José María Carrauco, 1852. Reprint of a letter to Guadalupe Victoria. (Sutro Library, San Francisco.)

Victoria, Guadalupe. [Oficio al Secretario de Estado y Relaciones Exponiendo las Causas de Disenciones Entre las Authoridades y Algunos Vecinos.] Veracruz, October 18, 1823. Signed by José Cacho, México, November 15, 1823. 1 leave. (HD 16-6.3491, Latin American Collection, University of Texas.)

Victoria, Guadalupe. [Carta a José Ignacio García Illueca sobre Dificultades de Proporcionar la Cantidad Debida a la Disposción de Iturbide.] Veracruz, April 22, 1823. 6 leaves. (HD 16-9.3733, Latin American Collection, University of Texas.)

Victoria, Guadalupe. [Carta al Secretario de Relaciones sobre la Fragata Contratada para el Transporte de Iturbide.] Veracruz, April 26, 1823. 1 leave. (HD 16-3.3285, Latin American Collection, University of Texas.)

Victoria, Guadalupe. [La Nación Mexicana. . . .] Primera Secretaria de Estado, Sección de Estado (head of letter). Palacio Nacional. México: 27 de Octubre de 1824. 5 leaves. A letter to Pope Leo XII outlining the aims of the new nation; and the hope that good relations would be fostered between the Catholic Church and the new government. (Latin American Collection, University of Texas.

MANUSCRIPTS

Bourdin, Bernardo. Papers, 1827-50. 1 v. Austin, Texas: University of Texas Library, Texas Archives (B 12/113, v. 722).

Butler, Anthony. Papers, 1810-1846. 1 foot. Austin, Texas: University of Texas Library, Texas Archives (A 4/34).

López de Santa Ana, Antonio. (Carta a Iturbide Sobre las Elecciones Municipales en Jalapa, Encomiendo Su

Regimiento y a Símismo, e Intimando Deslealtad del General Lobato y Sus Tropas.) Jalapa, Febrero 11, 1822. Austin, Texas: Hernández y Davolos Collection, University of Texas, Latin American Collection Library (HD 15-1.1537).

López de Santa Anna, Antonio. (Carta a Iturbide que no Puede Complir la Comisión de Recorrer por Su Salud la Costa de Sotavento en Busca del General Victoria; Propone a su Hermano; Advierte Peligro de Conspiracion Entre la Tropa Capitulada y el Coronel Márque, y Refiere las Dificultades Entre el General Dávila y el Sr. Liñan.) Austin, Texas: Hernández y Davalos Collection, University of Texas, Latin American Library (HD 15-2.1722). Jalapa, March 11, 1922.

Marcha, Capitan Don Pío. Carta . . . á Don Guadalupe Victoria ó Sea Contestación a Su Proclama: "A las Provincias de Oriente y Occidente." México: Imprenta de Ontiveras, 1823. British Museum: 9770. k.7 (29.).

Poinsett, Joel R. Letter to G. C. Sibley in the Valley of Taos, New Mexico. February 26, 1826. In regard to delays in making surveys due to U.S. presidential changes in administration. Western Historical Manuscipt Collection, University of Missouri Library: 1013, Box V, No. 17, 2 p.

Sibley, G. C. Letters to Benjamin H. Reeves and Thomas Mather. In reference to letter from Mr. Poinsett and appropriations to complete boundary surveys. Western Historical Manuscript Collection, University of Missouri Library: 1013, Box V, No. 28, 3 p.

El Supremo Poder Ejecutivo, Secretario del. (Borrador de Carta al General Guadalupe Victoria Sobre la Embarcación de Iturbide.) México: May 2, 1823. Austin, Texas: Hernández y Davalos Collection, University of Texas, Latin American Library (HD 16-3.3286).

Spain. Madrid. Real Academia de la Historia. Letters and Diaries of Don Juan Ruiz de Apodaca. Virrey de España en Nuevo Mexico. 20 September 1816 to 1821. 54 v. with index.

Spain. Archivo General de Indias. Sevilla. Audencia de México. Seccion Quinta, Vol. 1482, Estante 90, Cajon 1, Legajo 19. Letter from Félix María Calleja al Ministro de Gracia y Justicia, Mexico 18 Agosto de 1814. Regarding the continuing strength of the insurgents and the problems of getting financing and supplies.

--------, Legajo 39. A large amount of correspondence and documentation consisting of twenty pages giving information about various insurgent leaders; the establishment of the Congress in Chilpanzingo;

setting up of a Poder Ejecutivo and discussion of the Sentimientos de la Nacion written by Morelos.

PERIODICAL REFERENCES

Baur, John E. "The Evolution of a Mexican Foreign Trade Policy, 1821-1828." The Americas, Vol. XIX, January, 1963, No. 3, pp. 225-261.

Benson, Nettie Lee. "The Plan of Case Mata." The Hispanic American Historical Review, Vol. XXV, February, 1945, pp. 45-56.

Costeloe, Michael P. "Guadalupe Victoria and a Personal Loan from the Church in Independent Mexico." The Americas, Vol. XXV, January, 1969, No. 3, pp. 223-246.

Flaccus, Elmer W. "Guadalupe Victoria: His Personality as a Cause of His Failure." The Americas, Vol. XXIII, January 19, 1967, No. 3, pp. 297-311.

Greenleaf, Richard E. "The Mexican Inquisition and the Masonic Movement: 1751-1820." New Mexico Historical Review, Vol. XLIV, No. 2, 1969, pp. 94-117.

News items taken from the Niles Register:
Vol. 24, #608, p. 149, May 10, 1823.
Vol. 25, #638, p. 213, December 6, 1823.
Vol. 28, #710, pp. 125-128, April 23, 1825
Vol. 29, #733, pp. 79-80, October 1, 1825.
Vol. 30, #773, pp. 540-541, July 8, 1826.
Vol. 30, #775, pp. 368-369, July 22, 1826.
Vol. 32, #812, pp. 104-106, April 7, 1827.
Vol. 33, #833, p. 13, September 1, 1827.
Vol. 34, #881, p. 121, August 2, 1828.

Valdiosira Berman, Ramón. "Gobernantes de México." Artes de México, Año XXI, No. 174, 1974, pp. 3-98.

Valle, Rafael. "Consumación de Independencia" y "Iturbide, Varon de Dios." Artes de México, Año XVIII, 1971, pp. 4-104.

INDEX

Professor Arthur Leon DeVolder is Special Projects Director at the University of New Mexico's General Library, Albuquerque, New Mexico. He is a graduate of Indiana University with a degree in Public Business Administration, received his graduate degree in Library Science from the University of Denver, and his M.A. in Government and Citizenship from the University of New Mexico.

His publications in various periodicals range from library science to reading for youth and children, Hopi kachina dolls, and woodworking. His interest in Mexican history was sparked by Drs. Dorothy Woodward and Miguel Jorrin while he was a student at the University of New Mexico and by later subsequent travels to Mexico while at the University the past sixteen years.

Photo by the University
of New Mexico Photo Service